The Magic of Simple Signing

A Comprehensive Guide to Integrating Signs into Your Curriculum and Daily Life

First Edition

Jennifer Stewart Ms.Ed.

SIGNING courses

COMMUNICATION FOR ALL

FREE with Your Purchase!

Get exclusive access to:

- Sign Language Membership – Courses & LIVE support to guide you every step of the way
- ASL Materials – Instant digital downloads for your classroom or home
- Engaging Activities – Designed to help you start signing today!

Find out *how* in the activities section and begin your signing journey now!

Table of Contents

How To Use This Book

Dear Educators and Parents,

This book is for you—the teachers, caregivers, and parents who dedicate yourselves to shaping young minds, fostering communication, and creating inclusive spaces where every child has a voice. Whether you are in a classroom, a therapy setting, or your own home, you are your child's first and most important educator.

To the educators who pour your hearts into teaching, adapting, and finding ways to reach every child—*I see you*. You are the ones who believe in the power of language, who recognize that every child deserves the ability to express themselves, and who go above and beyond to provide the tools for success. Your work matters. This book is here to support you with practical strategies, research-backed insights, and a structured framework that will help you bring signing into your classroom with confidence and ease.

To the parents who spend every day nurturing, guiding, and advocating for your child—this book is for you, too. You are your child's first teacher, their safe place, and their most consistent source of love and communication. Whether you are here because you want to help your preverbal child express their needs, create a language-rich environment, or support a Deaf child in their linguistic development, know this:

You are giving your child a gift—the ability to be heard, understood, and connected in a meaningful way.

As a mother, educator, and daughter of a Deaf father, I know firsthand how powerful signing can be. I have seen the way one simple sign can open up a world of possibility for a child who is struggling to communicate. I have witnessed the joy on a parent's face when their child signs "more" or "love you" for the first time. I have watched teachers light up as they see their students thrive with an inclusive approach to language.

This book is not just about teaching signs—it's about creating connections, building relationships, and giving every child the ability to express their thoughts, emotions, and needs in a way that works for them. Whether you are here to help a Deaf child access their full linguistic rights, to introduce signing to a hearing child who is still developing speech, or to create a more inclusive learning environment—you are making a difference.

I have written this book as a clear, easy-to-follow guide, blending practical strategies with structured lesson plans so you have everything you need to scaffold your knowledge into a Simple Signs Curriculum.

At the end of this book, you'll find 240+ Simple Signing activities designed to make learning ASL fun and engaging. To ensure you can reuse these activities year after year, we recommend making copies of the pages. We've also included customizable templates, allowing you to create your own signing activities that best fit your needs.

As a special addition, you'll receive a Certificate of Completion—a proud symbol of your commitment to making sign language a part of your home, classroom, or program. Hang it on your door, display it in your space, and celebrate the progress you've made in fostering a signing-inclusive environment.

Thank you for being here.
Thank you for believing in the power of language and communication.
Thank you for being the educator, parent, and advocate that a child in your life needs.

Happy Signing!

Jennifer Stewart

Chapter 1: The Power of Simple Signing

Sign language is one of the most powerful tools for communication and early language development. Yet, many parents and educators hesitate to use it because they believe it is only meant for Deaf children. The truth is, signing benefits ALL children—not just those who are Deaf or hard of hearing.

In this chapter, we'll explore why signing is so impactful, how it helps children of all abilities, and why it is a gift from the Deaf community that should be embraced in every home and classroom.

In this chapter you will learn how signing:

- Reduces frustration – When children can sign *more, eat, all done*, they can express their needs without tantrums.
- Supports language development – Research shows that signing strengthens verbal language skills instead of replacing them.
- Creates stronger parent-child bonds – Signing gives parents and caregivers insight into what a child is thinking and feeling.
- Helps neurodiverse children – Signing is a lifeline for children with speech delays, autism, or other communication challenges.

"Tell me and I forget, teach me and I may remember, involve me and I learn."
Benjamin Franklin

Language is at the heart of human connection. It is how we express our thoughts, needs, emotions, and experiences. At the beginning of every semester, I ask my class, "Other than food, water, and shelter, what is the most important thing every child needs?" I believe the answer is communication because communication is human connection. For children, especially those who are still developing verbal skills, the inability to express themselves can be frustrating. This is where signing becomes invaluable.

Sign language isn't just for Deaf children—it's a powerful tool that helps all children communicate, build relationships, and develop stronger language skills. Many parents and educators worry that using signs will delay speech or that it's too complicated to incorporate into daily life. But the truth is, signing simplifies communication, enhances learning, and creates deeper connections between children and their caregivers.

The Benefits of Simple Signing

Signing isn't just about learning hand movements—it's about prompting communication before spoken words are fully developed. Children's brains are wired for language, but their vocal cords and motor skills take time to catch up. By introducing signs, we give them a way to communicate effectively before they can speak.

1. Signing Reduces Frustration

One of the biggest struggles for young children is not being understood. Imagine feeling hungry, tired, or wanting a favorite toy but not being able to tell anyone. This is a daily experience for many preverbal children, leading to tantrums, tears, and frustration.

When children have access to signs, even just a handful of basic ones like *more, eat, help,* and *all done*, they can clearly express their needs instead of crying or acting out. Instead of screaming at the dinner table, a child can simply sign *more* when they want another serving. Instead of throwing a toy in frustration, they can sign *help* when they need assistance.

The relief on a child's face when they realize they can communicate and be understood is incredible. It fosters confidence and reduces stress for both the child and the adult.

---

2. Signing Supports Language Development

One of the most common misconceptions is that signing will delay speech development, but research shows the opposite is true. Signing supports and enhances verbal language skills rather than replacing them.

When children sign, they are actively engaging their brains in language processing. Pairing signs with spoken words strengthens both receptive and expressive language skills, making it easier for children to transition to verbal communication when they're ready.

Multiple studies have shown that babies and toddlers who use sign language tend to:

- Learn to speak earlier than non-signing peers
- Show stronger reading skills later in life
- Have larger vocabularies by preschool age

Signing gives children a head start in language acquisition while also reinforcing speech development.

---

3. Signing Strengthens Parent-Child and Teacher-Student Bonds

One of the most beautiful things about signing is that it deepens the relationship between caregivers and children. Communication isn't just about exchanging words—it's about understanding and connection.

When a parent or educator signs with a child, they are actively engaging, making eye contact, and being present. Signing encourages more face-to-face interaction, which builds trust, emotional security, and a stronger bond between the adult and child.

For teachers, signing helps create a more inclusive and responsive classroom. Instead of relying solely on verbal cues, teachers who use signs can:

- Give clearer instructions
- Offer visual support for transitions and routines
- Help children express their needs without disrupting the class

In a world that often feels rushed, signing slows us down and encourages intentional communication—something that benefits all relationships.

---

4. Signing Helps Neurodiverse Children

For children who are neurodiverse—such as those with autism, apraxia, Down syndrome, or other speech delays—signing can be a lifeline. Many children with communication challenges struggle with spoken language processing, and having a visual, motor-based way to communicate can make all the difference.

Signing provides:

- A predictable and structured way to communicate
- A visual and kinesthetic language, which can be easier for some children than verbal speech
- A way to reduce anxiety by giving children an alternative method of expression

Many therapists and speech-language pathologists use signing as a bridge to verbal language for children who have delays in speech development. Even if a child never becomes fully verbal, signing provides an independent, reliable method of communication that improves their quality of life. We show you exactly how to do this using the Signing Courses Method.

My Foster Son and the Power of Signing

I'll never forget the moment my foster son first signed *all done*.

He had been with us for a few days, and communication was a constant struggle. It wasn't that he didn't know some signs, it was that he was too scared to use them. Just as children shut off verbally, they can also shut off all forms of communication– if scared enough. He was frustrated, and withdrawn, often acting out because he didn't know how to express his needs. He had experienced trauma, and verbal communication didn't come easily to him yet.

I knew that signing could help, but I wasn't sure how long it would take for him to pick it up. So I started modeling simple signs in our daily routines—showing him *more* during mealtimes, *help* when I assisted him with tasks, *all done* when we finished an activity. It turns out that he had some access to signs before he came to us. The more comfortable he became, the more signs we saw.

At first, he just watched, not really indicating he knew any sign language. Then, one evening, while trying to put on his shoes, he struggled, huffed in frustration, and looked up at me. And instead of crying or throwing the shoe, he raised his hands and signed help while muttering a vague "elp" to accompany the sign.

It was a small moment, but it felt huge. His whole body relaxed as I signed back, "Oh! You need help!" and bent down to assist him. The relief on his face was undeniable—for the first time in a long time, he felt safe enough to communicate, and thanks to sign language, he was heard.

From that moment, everything started to shift. He began using signs daily, which reduced his meltdowns, increased his confidence, and built our bond in ways I hadn't imagined. We are grateful his caregiver before us knew enough to introduce signs to him. By age two, our foster son was speaking in full sentences and no longer needed speech therapy. He is two and half now and still uses his first signs for emphasis within his full spoken language. For example, when he *really* wants something, he will communicate verbally and sign *please* for emphasis.

That moment reaffirmed for me what I already knew: signing is more than just a tool—it's a bridge to connection, understanding, and trust.

And that is the magic of simple signing.

Chapter 2: Understanding ASL vs. Gestures and the Dangers of Language Deprevation

Many people assume that signs and gestures are interchangeable. However, ASL is a fully developed language with its own grammar, syntax, and cultural significance.

- Gestures are informal and vary from person to person (e.g., waving, pointing).
- ASL Signs follow a structured linguistic system and remain consistent across users.

Using ASL rather than random gestures gives children access to a true language that can grow with them as they develop.

In this chapter, we'll explore:

- The five parameters of a sign and what makes a sign a sign
- How ASL functions as a language
- The key differences between ASL and gestures
- Why using real signs is important for a child's linguistic growth
- The cognitive benefits of learning a structured language like ASL
- What Language Deprivation is and how we can prevent it.

"The principal goal of education is to create individuals who are capable of doing new things, not simply repeating what other generations have done." Jean Piaget (Child Psychologist and Cognitive Development Theorist)

One of the biggest misunderstandings about sign language is the assumption that it is simply a set of hand gestures or pantomime that anyone can make up on the spot. In reality, American Sign Language (ASL) is a fully developed language with its own complex grammar, syntax, and linguistic structure.

This misconception is widespread, even among professionals working in early childhood education and speech therapy. Many well-meaning educators and caregivers create made-up hand movements to help children communicate, assuming that any physical gesture is just as effective as a sign. However, there is a significant difference between a gesture and a true ASL sign—and using actual ASL signs rather than informal gestures provides children with access to a real, structured language that enhances cognitive and linguistic development.

The Five Parameters of a Sign: What Makes a Sign a Sign?

Every spoken language has rules that determine how words are formed, structured, and used. English, for example, follows rules of grammar, phonetics, and sentence structure. Similarly, ASL has specific linguistic rules that govern how signs are formed and understood.

Every ASL sign consists of five parameters:

1. **Handshape** – The shape the hand takes when forming a sign.
2. **Palm Orientation** – The direction the palm faces during a sign.
3. **Location** – Where the sign is produced on the body or in signing space.
4. **Movement** – The motion used to create the sign.
5. **Non-Manual Signals (NMS)** – Facial expressions, mouth movements, or body shifts that modify the meaning of the sign.

If even one of these parameters is changed, the meaning of the sign can change completely—just as changing a sound in a spoken word can alter its meaning.

For example:

- The signs for mother and father have the same handshape and movement but are produced in different locations (chin vs. forehead).
- The signs for help and help-yourself have the same handshape and location but differ in movement.
- The sign for not yet and late use the same handshape, movement, and location, but the non-manual signal (a head tilt with tongue out) changes the meaning.

This is why ASL signs cannot be randomly substituted with gestures—they follow specific linguistic rules that must be understood and maintained for accurate communication.

ASL vs. Gestures: The Critical Differences

A gesture is a spontaneous body movement used to express an idea or feeling. Examples include:

- Pointing to indicate direction
- Waving hello or goodbye
- Shrugging to indicate confusion
- Giving a thumbs-up for approval

While gestures are useful for basic communication, they lack the structure, grammar, and linguistic depth of a true language.

Key Differences Between ASL and Gestures:

Feature	American Sign Language (ASL)	Gestures
Grammar	Has a defined grammatical structure, including syntax, morphology, and rules.	No grammar—gestures are often random and informal.
Vocabulary	ASL signs have established meanings and can be used in full conversations.	Gestures are often ambiguous and open to interpretation.
Consistency	ASL is standardized and understood by millions of people.	Gestures vary widely by culture, context, and individuals.
Linguistic Depth	ASL has morphology, syntax, and sentence structure like spoken languages.	Gestures lack linguistic rules or formal structure.
Cognitive Benefits	Learning ASL improves brain development, memory, and problem-solving.	Gestures don't have the same neurological impact

Why Using Real Signs Matters for a Child's Linguistic Growth

Many educators and parents unknowingly create their own hand signs instead of using ASL. They assume that as long as a child understands the gesture, it's just as effective as a sign. However, research has shown that exposure to a structured language like ASL provides significantly greater cognitive and linguistic benefits than using gestures alone.

Language Acquisition and Brain Development

Research in neurolinguistics has shown that learning a structured language like ASL activates the same cognitive areas of the brain as learning a spoken language. When a child is exposed to ASL, they develop stronger neural connections that:

- Enhance memory retention
- Improve executive function and problem-solving skills
- Increase language fluency in both signed and spoken languages

When a child learns made-up gestures, they are not accessing a real linguistic system. This limits their ability to develop advanced language skills and means they must later "unlearn" the gestures and replace them with real signs if they ever transition to ASL.

Cognitive and Social Benefits of Learning ASL Over Gestures

Beyond communication, learning ASL provides numerous cognitive and social advantages that gestures do not.

1. Bilingual Brain Boost

ASL is a visual-spatial language, which activates different areas of the brain than spoken languages. Research has shown that bilingual children (including those who learn sign language) demonstrate stronger problem-solving skills and mental flexibility.

2. Enhanced Memory and Learning

Because ASL engages motor, visual, and linguistic memory simultaneously, children who sign tend to:

- Learn new words faster
- Develop better reading skills

- Retain information more effectively

3. Increased Social Inclusion

Using real ASL signs instead of gestures makes communication more inclusive. Children who learn ASL can communicate with Deaf peers and adults, opening doors to greater social interaction and inclusivity.

Language Deprivation: The Silent Crisis in Early Childhood Development

Language deprivation is a serious and often irreversible condition that occurs when a child is not given sufficient exposure to a fully accessible language during their critical language development years (birth to age five).

For Deaf children, language deprivation happens when they are not exposed to sign language early enough, leading to delays in cognitive, social, and academic development. For hearing children, deprivation can occur if they lack rich language interactions in their early years, leading to speech and literacy delays.

Language deprivation occurs when a child is not exposed to a fully accessible, structured language during their early developmental years.

1. For Deaf children, this happens when they are denied exposure to sign language and expected to rely solely on spoken language and lip reading, despite the fact that they cannot fully access spoken language auditorily.
2. For hearing children, language deprivation occurs when they are not spoken to, engaged with, or provided a rich language environment, leading to delays in speech, literacy, and social communication skills.

The Critical Period for Language Development

The first five years of life are the most crucial time for brain development, especially when it comes to language. If a child does not have sufficient exposure to language during this period, their ability to acquire and use language fluently can be permanently affected.

Research in neurolinguistics has shown that language is time-sensitive—after a certain point, the brain loses its ability to fully acquire and process language if it has not been exposed to one.

Dr. Laura Ann Petitto, a cognitive neuroscientist specializing in language acquisition, found that:

- The brain's language pathways develop optimally between birth and age five.
- The brain requires natural language input (signed or spoken) to develop linguistic structures properly.
- Children who are deprived of language during this window may never achieve full fluency in any language.

This means that if a child is not exposed to a full language—whether ASL or a spoken language—by the age of five, their brain will struggle to ever fully acquire language.

Language Deprivation in Deaf Children

The Deaf community refers to language deprivation as a human rights crisis because many Deaf children are denied access to sign language, leading to significant cognitive and academic delays.

How Language Deprivation Occurs in Deaf Children

Despite decades of research showing that ASL is the most accessible language for Deaf children, many medical professionals and educators still discourage parents from using sign language with their Deaf children.

Common causes of language deprivation in Deaf children:

- **Oralism and Speech-Only Education** – Deaf children are expected to learn spoken language through lip-reading and speech therapy, despite the fact that only 30-40% of spoken English is visible on the lips.
- **Delaying ASL Until After Cochlear Implantation** – Many parents are told to wait and see how well their child responds to a cochlear implant before introducing sign language, causing months or years of language deprivation.
- **Lack of Early Intervention** – Many Deaf children do not receive language support in the critical years when the brain is most primed for language acquisition.
- **Seeing ASL as Gestures and not as a True Language** – As we stated in this chapter, too many individuals still confuse ASL for gestures which takes away the value and meaning of what ASL gives to children- *language*.

The Consequences of Language Deprivation for Deaf Children

Children who experience language deprivation often suffer from:

1. Cognitive delays – The brain struggles to develop fully without early language input.
2. Low literacy rates – Deaf children who do not learn ASL early often have poor reading skills because English is difficult to acquire without a solid first language.
3. Social-emotional struggles – Without language, children struggle to build relationships, express emotions, and develop self-identity.

A groundbreaking 2017 study by linguists Mayberry, Kluender, and Neville showed that:

- Deaf children who learn ASL from birth have cognitive skills equal to their hearing peers.
- Deaf children who do not learn sign language early struggle with academic and linguistic fluency for life.
- Even Deaf children who receive cochlear implants benefit from learning ASL alongside spoken language.

Language Deprivation in Hearing Children

While language deprivation is more widely discussed in Deaf education, it can also occur in hearing children if they are not exposed to consistent, interactive language experiences early in life.

How Language Deprivation Occurs in Hearing Children

- **Lack of verbal interaction** – When parents or caregivers do not talk, read, or engage with their child in meaningful ways, the child does not receive enough language input.
- **Excessive screen time replacing conversation** – Research shows that young children learn language through direct human interaction, not from passive screen exposure.
- **Neglect or limited social engagement** – Children who are raised in neglectful environments or have caregivers who do not engage in conversation may experience severe speech delays.

The Consequences of Language Deprivation for Hearing Children

A 2018 study by Hart and Risley found that by age four:

- Children from language-rich households hear up to 30 million more words than children from language-deprived environments.

- Children with low language exposure struggle with vocabulary, reading, and school readiness.

Long-term effects of early language deprivation in hearing children:

1. Delayed speech and limited vocabulary
2. Struggles with reading and literacy development
3. Reduced social skills and communication difficulties

The Importance of Signing for Language Development in ALL Children

Sign language is one of the most effective tools for preventing language deprivation because it provides a visual, accessible means of communication from infancy.

- For Deaf children, ASL ensures full language access from birth.
- For hearing children, signing enhances language development and prevents delays.

The brain doesn't distinguish between spoken and signed languages—it simply needs language input to develop properly. Dr. Laura Ann Petitto's research on bilingual language acquisition found that:

- Children exposed to both sign language and spoken language develop cognitive advantages over monolingual children.
- The human brain is wired to acquire language visually just as efficiently as auditorily.
- Signing provides a strong foundation for literacy and verbal fluency.

By using ASL with children, we are preventing language deprivation and ensuring that every child, regardless of hearing ability, has access to full language development.

My Father's Journey to Language

My father, Dr. David Stewart, was born into a world that would not grant him language easily. He was a bright and curious child, but at the age of four, his world changed forever. Meningitis took his hearing, leaving him and his sister Deaf in a family that had no way of understanding what that truly meant.

His parents were immigrants from the Poland-Ukraine region, having settled in Canada in search of a better life. But their struggles as newcomers—learning a new country, a new culture, and a new language—left no room for them to learn about Deafness or American Sign Language (ASL). They did not know how to teach their Deaf children to communicate, and they were never told that there was a language perfectly suited for them.

Instead, my father and his sister were expected to speak, lip-read, and function in a hearing world without the linguistic tools to do so.

My grandmother, determined to get my father to talk, developed her own method of speech training: bribery. If he and his sister could say words correctly, they would get candy. She would hold up a sweet treat and encourage them to repeat sounds and words, rewarding them when they got close enough.

This became their first experience with structured language, but it was slow and fragmented. There were gaps in communication, frustration, and a sense that something was always missing.

But my father was brilliant in ways that went beyond speech. He understood math. Numbers were written, visual and universal, and they made sense to him in a way that spoken words did not. He could solve problems, recognize patterns, and make sense of the world in ways that had nothing to do with sound.

Still, without full access to language, his world remained small and constrained. Then, in high school, everything changed. He was introduced to ASL. For the first time in his life, language was not a struggle. It was not about straining to hear, trying to lip-read, or guessing at the meaning of words. Instead, it was visual, fluid, expressive, and completely accessible. His world opened up.

With ASL, he could have real conversations. He could express abstract thoughts, deep emotions, and complex ideas without limits. And he never stopped learning. ASL gave my father the foundation he needed to thrive—not just as a Deaf individual, but as a scholar, an innovator, and a leader in the Deaf community.

Once my father had full access to language, he devoted his life to ensuring that no Deaf child would have to struggle the way he did.

His career was groundbreaking. He became:

1. **The Director of the Deaf Education Program**, shaping the way Deaf education was taught and studied.
2. **A Bestselling Author**, writing countless books on Deaf education, ASL, and Deaf culture—books that are still used in classrooms today.
3. An **Award-Winning Inventor**, creating the **first-ever fully online, on-demand ASL program**, paving the way for digital Deaf education.
4. **A Trailblazer for Deaf Scholars**, proving that Deaf individuals belong in academia and research.
5. **A Father of Four**, raising a family while dedicating his life to Deaf advocacy.
6. **A Coach for the Canadian Deaf Olympics Team**, mentoring Deaf athletes and showing the world what Deaf people could achieve.

He did all this and so much more. Through his work, he paved the way for future generations of Deaf educators, researchers, and leaders. His contributions shaped Deaf education as we know it today, and his books continue to educate and inspire those who seek to understand ASL, Deaf culture, and the importance of language accessibility.

What my father achieved was remarkable—not because he was Deaf, but because he was finally given access to language. His story is proof of something that should never have been questioned in the first place: Language is not a privilege. It is a right. And when Deaf children are given full, unrestricted access to language—whether through ASL, bilingual education, or early intervention—their potential is limitless.

His legacy lives on in the books he wrote, the students he taught, the Deaf educators he mentored, the technology he pioneered, and the lives he changed. Because of him, the world is a better place for Deaf children, Deaf scholars, and the future of ASL education.

Chapter 3: The Seven Steps to Integrating Signing – The Signing Courses Method

Successfully implementing sign language in your home or classroom doesn't have to be overwhelming. Here are the seven steps to get started:

The Seven Steps to Signing Success:

1. **Learn** – Understand the sign and what it may look like when a child uses it.
2. **Teach** – Educate others so that everyone interacting with the child is consistent.
3. **Introduce** – Begin incorporating the sign in daily interactions.
4. **Encourage** – Support the child in initiating the sign independently.
5. **Acknowledge** – Recognize and reinforce the child's attempts.
6. **Patience** – Allow time for learning without rushing the process.
7. **Repeat** – Reinforce the sign consistently and introduce new ones when ready.

By following these simple, effective steps, you can build a signing-friendly environment that benefits all learners.

"Language is the instrument of expressing and not merely of communicating thought."
Maria Montessori (Educator and Founder of the Montessori Method)

When introducing sign language to children, consistency, intentionality, and engagement are key. The Signing Courses Method is designed to ensure that signs are introduced properly, making signing a natural and effective part of communication.

This structured approach helps educators, caregivers, and parents successfully integrate signing into their daily interactions with children. It guarantees that signs are introduced in a way that ensures understanding, retention, and independent use.

These seven steps provide a proven framework for incorporating signs into the classroom and home environment. For educators, these steps can be incorporated seamlessly into the classroom environment. The following sections provide real-life classroom examples and practical strategies for applying each step in an educational setting.

Step 1: Learn

Before expecting children to learn a sign, you must first learn it yourself.

This means understanding:

- The correct ASL handshape, movement, location, and palm orientation
- How a child's developing motor skills may cause modifications of the sign
- How to naturally incorporate the sign into daily routines

Classroom Example:

A teacher wants to introduce the sign "sit" for classroom transitions.

1. She first looks at the Signing Courses posters or flashcards, or online video support to learn the correct sign.
2. She practices the sign in a mirror to ensure clarity.

3. She observes how toddlers might modify the sign (e.g., making a simple downward motion instead of forming the correct handshape).

4. She takes the Signing Courses poster or flashcard with the ASL sign and places it by the circle time area.

Additional Tip for Educators:

- Use ASL video resources to ensure accuracy. The National Association of the Deaf (NAD) and Signing Courses offer great tools.
- Practice with another teacher to get comfortable before introducing the sign to students.

Step 2: Teach

Once the sign is learned, everyone who interacts with the child should know it too.

This step ensures consistency in signing across different environments, including:

- Teachers in the classroom
- Teacher's assistants or aides
- Speech therapists or interventionists
- Parents and caregivers

Classroom Example:

A teacher introduces the sign "help" to her class.

1. She teaches her assistant and other staff members the sign.
2. She sends a video home to parents so they can reinforce it at home.
3. She explains to students that they can use the sign whenever they need help instead of calling out.
4. She posts a visual reminder of the sign at different learning stations.

Additional Tip for Educators:

- Host a mini-training session with staff to introduce common classroom signs. Signing Courses offers parent workshops.
- Provide parents with take-home flashcards so they can reinforce signing at home.

Step 3: Introduce

Now that everyone understands the sign, it's time to incorporate it into real-life classroom interactions.

This means using the sign:

- Every time the corresponding word is spoken
- In structured classroom routines
- In spontaneous moments when the sign naturally fits

Classroom Example:

A teacher introduces the sign "stop" during classroom movement activities.

1. During circle time, she sings a song where students must stop and go. She signs and says "stop" each time.
2. During recess, she models the sign when she tells students to stop running.
3. She pauses to allow students to sign "stop" themselves before continuing an activity.

Additional Tip for Educators:

- Use music and movement activities to make signing more engaging.

- Reinforce signs through daily classroom jobs (e.g., one child can be the "sign leader" for the day).

Step 4: Encourage

Now that the sign is part of the classroom routine, students should be encouraged to use it themselves.

Encouragement should be:

- Natural and pressure-free
- Modeled often
- Paired with positive reinforcement

Classroom Example:

A teacher encourages children to sign "more" at snack time.

1. She waits before immediately giving refills, giving children a moment to attempt the sign.
2. If a child points instead of signing, she models the correct sign while saying, "I see you want more! Let's sign 'more' together!"
3. She reinforces efforts, even if the sign is not perfect.

Additional Tip for Educators:

- Pair signs with classroom jobs (e.g., students sign "more" when they need extra supplies).
- Celebrate every signing attempt with a smile, praise, or high-five!

Step 5: Acknowledge

Acknowledgment helps children build confidence in signing.

- Recognize signing attempts—even if they're imperfect
- Reinforce effort with enthusiasm and excitement
- Create a positive environment where signing is encouraged

Classroom Example:

A teacher is teaching the sign "thank you".

1. When a child signs a close approximation (like touching their chin but not fully extending the hand), she responds, "Wow! You signed 'thank you!' That's amazing!"
2. She then models the correct sign and encourages the child to do it again.

Additional Tip for Educators:

- Use stickers or small rewards for signing efforts.
- Create a signing wall of achievement where students' names go up when they learn new signs.

Step 6: Patience

Signing is a skill that takes time. Children may need weeks or months before consistently using a sign.

Classroom Example:

A teacher introduces the sign "wait" and models it daily. At first, none of the children sign back.

Instead of giving up, she:

- Continues modeling the sign every day during transitions.
- Uses repetition without pressure.
- Celebrates even small attempts (like a hand movement close to the correct sign).

Additional Tip for Educators:

- Be patient! Signing takes time.
- Don't force it—keep signing, and the child will eventually follow!

Step 7: Repeat

Repetition is key to success. Once one sign is mastered, repeat the process with new signs!

Classroom Example:

A teacher starts with three signs: more, eat, and help. Once the children use them consistently, she gradually adds new signs like sit, play, and share.

She repeats the entire Signing Courses Method with each new sign.

Additional Tip for Educators:

- Introduce 1-2 signs at a time and build from there.
- Keep signing FUN and engaging!

Examples of How to Use The Signing Courses Method at Home

Step 1: Learn

- Watch an Signing Courses video tutorial on the sign "more" and practice in front of a mirror before using it with your child.
- Observe how toddlers modify signs (e.g., clapping instead of forming "more") to recognize early attempts.

Step 2: Teach

- Show grandparents and babysitters the sign "more" so they can reinforce it at mealtime.
- Make a simple ASL chart on the fridge with pictures of the signs your family is using. Use Signing Courses posters or flashcards to help create your own visuals.

Step 3: Introduce

- During bath time, sign and say "water" every time your child splashes.
- Sign "sleep" each night while tucking your child into bed.

Step 4: Encourage

- When your child reaches for a snack, pause and say, "I see you want 'more'!" while modeling the sign.
- If your child attempts to sign "help" but does it incorrectly, respond enthusiastically and sign back, "Yes! You're asking for help!"

Step 5: Acknowledge

- If your child signs "all done" at the dinner table, clap and say, "You signed all done! That's amazing!"
- When they use any signing attempt, immediately respond by fulfilling the request (e.g., giving more food when they sign "more").

Step 6: Patience

- If your child doesn't sign back yet, continue modeling the sign without pressure (e.g., signing "milk" every time you offer a bottle).
- Allow time for natural learning—some children may take weeks before using a sign regularly.

Step 7: Repeat

- After your child masters "more", start introducing "please" using the same steps.
- Reinforce learned signs daily by integrating them into normal routines, like signing "bath" before heading to the tub.

How My Daughter Inspired The Signing Courses Method

When my daughter was born, I knew I wanted to introduce sign language to her right away. I had seen firsthand how signing benefited young children—reducing frustration, increasing communication, and strengthening bonds between caregivers and babies. But when I actually started signing with her, I realized something: there was no clear, structured way to introduce signs effectively.

I tried different methods, watched what worked and what didn't, and through trial and error, the Signing Courses Method was born. It wasn't just about showing a sign once or twice and hoping she'd pick it up. It was about being intentional, consistent, and patient. And now, that same method has successfully taught thousands of children of all ages and abilities to sign.

I will never forget the moment my daughter signed "milk" for the first time. She was just five months old—barely sitting up on her own, still in that adorable baby stage where every new expression felt like a discovery.

I had been signing "milk" to her every time I nursed or gave her a bottle. I didn't expect her to sign back yet—I was just modeling, following the steps of what would later become the Signing Courses Method. But one day, she looked up at me, made a small fist opening and closing, and stared intently, waiting.

It wasn't an accident. She wasn't randomly moving her hands. She had connected the sign to meaning—and she was telling me she wanted milk.

I nearly jumped with excitement! "Oh my goodness, yes, milk!" I said, immediately feeding her while signing it back. That was it—her first real, intentional communication. She knew what she wanted, and she knew how to ask for it. At five months old, my baby was already using language to express her needs.

Her second sign was "sleep", and this one made an even bigger impact on our daily lives. By six months old, she would sign "sleep" when she was tired. And get this—she wasn't just letting us know she was sleepy. She would put herself to sleep. Let me tell you, the reactions from other parents were priceless.

We would be out with friends, chatting while holding our babies, when my daughter would sign "sleep", snuggle into my chest, and just doze off—peacefully, effortlessly, on her own. No crying, no rocking, no desperate attempts to get her to settle.

People would stare. I could feel the other parents watching, some of them a little jealous, others completely in awe. "How did you get her to do that??" they would ask. The answer? She knew she was safe. She knew we understood her. She knew she was in control of her own needs.

She didn't have to cry to communicate. She didn't have to fight sleep because she was unsure of what was happening. She had a language that connected her to us, and that language gave her security. I had always known signing worked, but this was next-level.

We made signing a natural part of our family life. My daughter wasn't the only one signing—her older brother signed too. He loved showing her signs and modeling them alongside us. This made a huge difference. She never questioned whether signing was something she should do because everyone around her was doing it. It wasn't just something "Mom does" or "Dad does"—it was how our family communicated.

By her first birthday, she was signing over 15 different words, and communication was seamless. She didn't have tantrums because she never had to. She could express herself, and we could understand her.

As my daughter grew, her language skills didn't just develop—they thrived. By the time she started speaking, she wasn't just learning English—she was learning Spanish too. And the most incredible part? Signing gave her the foundation to absorb multiple languages effortlessly.

At home, we spoke English. But when she started attending a Spanish immersion school, she picked up Spanish flawlessly. No hesitation, no confusion—just a smooth transition into a second language. I firmly believe that her early exposure to sign language is what made this possible. ASL had already taught her that language is visual, interactive, and expressive. It had strengthened her language-processing skills, making it easier for her brain to recognize, categorize, and acquire new languages.

Now, she speaks Spanish fluently at school and English at home—a bilingual child whose journey with language began with simple signs.

Early Signing Sets Children Up for Lifelong Success

The experience of teaching my daughter to sign changed everything for me. It showed me firsthand that signing isn't just about communication—it's about connection, confidence, and cognitive growth. From the first time she signed "milk", to the moment she peacefully signed "sleep", to watching her flourish as a bilingual learner, I knew: *Signing gives children an unmatched advantage in life*.

And that is why I created The Signing Courses Method—so that other families, educators, and caregivers can experience the same success, the same ease of communication, and the same incredible results that we did. Signing isn't just for Deaf children. It's for all children.

It opens the brain in ways that only sign language can, setting them up for success in communication, literacy, and even multilingual learning.

I have seen it work in thousands of children since my daughter, and I can tell you this:

- *Signing works.*
- *Signing reduces frustration.*
- *Signing strengthens cognitive skills.*
- *Signing gives children a head start in language learning.*

And most importantly—signing helps children feel understood. It all started with my daughter, and now, this method is changing the way children communicate all over the world.

Simple Signs Steps
Signing Courses Method for Signing Success

STEP 1: Learn

Learn how to do a sign and what the sign may look like when a child does it versus when you do.

STEP 2: Teach

Teach everyone who spends time with the child the signs you are using and what they may look like when a child signs them.

STEP 3: Introduce

Introduce by implementing. Use the sign in your daily routine by speaking and signing the word at the same time. Model the communication behavior you want to see.

STEP 4: Encourage

Encourage the child to initiate signs.

STEP 5: Acknowledge

Acknowledge when the child has demonstrated a solid attempt with signing.

STEP 6: Patience

Practice patience. Do not rush the signs.

STEP 7: Repeat

Repeat the sign from here on out. Repeat the method with new signs when ready.

This poster, along with over a dozen more are included in the package. Follow the prompts given in the activity section to get your digital download today.

Chapter 4: Why Early Signing Matters for All Children

Many people assume that sign language is only beneficial for Deaf and hard-of-hearing children or babies, but research and real-world experience tell us otherwise. Early exposure to sign language benefits all children, regardless of their hearing ability, learning style, or linguistic background.

From preverbal infants to bilingual learners, from neurodiverse children to those with speech delays, signing is a universal tool that strengthens communication, literacy, and cognitive development.

This chapter will explore:

- How signing enhances communication and reduces frustration
- Why signing supports early language development and literacy
- How sign language bridges the gap for bilingual learners, especially between home and school
- How signing supports neurodiverse and speech-delayed children

---

"There needs to be a lot more emphasis on what a child can do instead of what they cannot do." Temple Grandin (Autistic Scientist, Author, and Advocate)

Signing as a Bridge to Communication Before Speech Develops

Most people understand that babies and toddlers understand far more than they can express. Before speech develops, young children often experience frustration because they lack the words to communicate their needs. This is where early signing becomes a game-changer.

Imagine this scenario: A one-year-old child is sitting in a high chair, pointing toward the fridge and making noises, but their parent doesn't know exactly what they want. Are they hungry? Do they want milk? A snack? Now, picture the same child, but instead of pointing and fussing, they sign "milk."

The parent immediately understands and responds:

"Oh! You want milk?" (while signing "milk" back)

The child nods, excited that they were understood—without crying or frustration.

While many refer to this type of signing as "baby sign," it's best to avoid this label, as it reinforces the misconception that a child's signs are mere gestures rather than an early attempt at using the true language of ASL.

Research Insight

A 2000 study by Dr. Linda Acredolo and Dr. Susan Goodwyn found that babies who learned sign language had fewer tantrums, developed stronger bonds with caregivers, and showed advanced language skills by age two compared to non-signing peers.

Signing Strengthens Language and Literacy Development

One of the biggest misconceptions about signing is the belief that it delays speech development. In reality, research shows the opposite—children who learn sign language tend to have larger vocabularies, stronger literacy skills, and faster speech development than those who do not.

Signing reinforces spoken words by strengthening the connection between language and meaning. It engages visual, auditory, and motor memory, making learning more interactive and effective. Signing also teaches key literacy skills such as:

- **Sequencing** – Understanding the order of words and events in a sentence or story.
- **Comprehension** – Making meaningful connections between words, images, and concepts.
- **Association** – Recognizing that words, symbols, and signs are all representations of meaning.

When a child is learning a new word, they often need multiple forms of input to truly understand and retain it.

For example, a toddler learning the word "dog" might:

- Hear the word "dog" spoken aloud.
- See a picture of a dog in a book or on a flashcard.
- Sign "dog" by patting their leg.

This multi-sensory approach reinforces the connection between the word, its meaning, and how it is represented visually and kinesthetically. By engaging multiple learning pathways, signing helps children retain words faster and use them more confidently.

Research Insight

A 2003 study published in the *Journal of Speech, Language, and Hearing Research* found that:

- Children who were introduced to sign language at an early age had stronger reading comprehension skills than their non-signing peers.
- Signing enhances phonemic awareness, helping children recognize and understand how spoken words are formed.
- Sign language provides a bridge to written language, making it easier for children to transition into reading and spelling.

How Literacy Educators Can Use the Signing Courses Flashcards and Posters to Support Learning

The Signing Courses Flashcards and Posters are powerful tools for integrating ASL into literacy instruction. They help educators:

- Introduce new vocabulary in a multi-sensory way
- Reinforce sight words and high-frequency words through sign language
- Make reading lessons more interactive and engaging

Here are practical ways educators can use these resources in their classrooms:

1. Sign and Read: Matching Signs to Sight Words

Many young readers struggle with sight words because they cannot be sounded out phonetically. Pairing these words with ASL signs helps children remember them faster because they are connected to a physical movement and visual cue.

How to Use It:

- Select a set of sight words (e.g., *more, help, stop, play, see*).
- Show the Signing Courses Flashcard for each word, demonstrating the sign while saying the word.
- Have children say the word, sign it, and write it on a whiteboard to reinforce learning.

2. Using ASL in Storytelling and Read-Alouds

Adding signs while reading aloud helps children stay engaged while strengthening listening and comprehension skills.

How to Use It:

- Choose a book that includes words that have ASL signs (e.g., *Brown Bear, Brown Bear, What Do You See?*).
- Use the Signing Courses Posters to preview key signs before reading.
- As you read, pause to sign key words, encouraging students to sign along.

By actively participating in signing, children internalize words more effectively and build stronger language comprehension skills.

3. Signing for Phonemic Awareness and Spelling

Signing helps children break words down into smaller parts, supporting phonemic awareness and spelling.

How to Use It:

- Use the ASL alphabet chart from the Signing Courses Posters to introduce fingerspelling for letter recognition.
- Have students spell out short words (like cat, dog, sun) while signing each letter.
- Challenge students to say the word, sign the word, then spell the word aloud.

This process reinforces letter-sound relationships and makes spelling more interactive.

4. Signing as a Classroom Behavior Management Tool

Using signs in the classroom helps children follow directions, transition between activities, and communicate nonverbally when needed.

How to Use It:

- Teach the ASL signs for "stop," "wait," and "listen" at the beginning of the school year.
- Post the Signing Courses Posters around the classroom for visual reinforcement.
- Instead of raising their hands, allow children to use the "help" sign when they need assistance.

This method not only supports literacy but also encourages independence and self-regulation.

Using ASL as a Bridge for Bilingual Learners: Connecting Home and School

Many bilingual families face a language gap between what is spoken at home and what is used in the classroom. This transition can be challenging for young children, as they are expected to adapt to two different languages while still developing their communication skills.

The Signing Courses Method provides an easy way to connect home and school languages by using ASL as a bridge between spoken languages.

Step-by-Step Example: Using ASL to Transition Between Spanish and English

Step 1: Speak the Spanish word while signing in ASL

- During breakfast, a parent says "leche"(Spanish for milk) while signing "milk" in ASL.
- The child now associates the Spanish word with the ASL sign.

Step 2: Introduce the English word with the same ASL sign

- At daycare, the teacher uses the same ASL sign but says **"milk"** in English.
- The child recognizes the sign and understands that "milk" and "leche" mean the same thing.

Step 3: Transition to full bilingual use

- Over time, the child learns that the ASL sign represents the concept, making it easier to switch between Spanish and English naturally.

By following this method, ASL acts as a bridge between the two spoken languages, making the transition smoother and less confusing for young learners.

Real-Life Classroom Example

A teacher uses ASL to help Spanish-speaking students transition into an English-speaking classroom.

- He first teaches common classroom signs, such as "sit," "help," and "bathroom", while saying them in Spanish.
- Once the children understand the signs, he gradually transitions to saying the words in English while still using ASL.
- The students quickly associate the sign with both words, helping them grasp English faster without losing their Spanish foundation.

Using ASL in this way provides a consistent, visual cue that remains the same across languages, making learning more effective.

How Signing Helps Neurodiverse and Speech-Delayed Children

For children with autism, apraxia, Down syndrome, sensory processing disorders, and other developmental differences, sign language is one of the most effective tools for building communication skills. It is also invaluable for children with speech delays, as it allows them to express themselves while working on verbal speech at their own pace.

- Provides a multi-sensory approach by engaging visual, auditory, and motor processing
- Reduces communication-related frustration by offering an accessible way to express needs
- Strengthens brain connectivity for speech development by activating language centers
- Encourages joint attention and engagement, supporting social interaction

Research Insight

A study published in the *Journal of Autism and Developmental Disorders* found that children with autism who used sign language experienced fewer behavioral outbursts compared to those without access to signing.

- Start with need-based signs such as "more," "help," and "stop" to create routine-based communication.
- Pair ASL with verbal speech but do not require verbalization for the sign to be effective.
- Acknowledge all signing attempts, even if they are not perfect.
- Reinforce signing across multiple environments (home, school, therapy).

Sign language provides a bridge to communication, reducing frustration and empowering children to express themselves in a way that feels natural to them.

The Student Who Had the Gift of Deafness

I will never forget the time I spent working in an ASD (Autism Spectrum Disorder) classroom as an ASL interpreter. It was a room filled with students who had a range of abilities and challenges—many with severe speech delays, cognitive impairments, emotional disorders, and sensory processing difficulties.

Among them was one student who stood out—not because of his disabilities, but because of what he had that the others didn't: a fully accessible language.

He was Deaf and blind, and he also had cognitive delays, an emotional disorder, and multiple developmental challenges. On paper, he would have been considered the most impaired student in the room—but in reality, he was the most linguistically advanced. He had sign language.

AAC Devices: A Tool, Not the Full Solution

Every other student in the class relied on AAC (Augmentative and Alternative Communication) devices to communicate. These were incredible tools that helped bridge the gap for students who could not speak. But they had limitations—they were only part of the solution, not the whole answer.

AAC devices:

- Require programming – A teacher or caregiver has to input phrases and words, meaning the student can only communicate what has been pre-programmed.
- Lack spontaneity – If a student has a thought that isn't programmed into the device, they cannot express it in real time.
- Depend on technology – Devices run out of battery, malfunction, or require repairs. When that happens, communication stops.

But this Deaf student? He didn't need an AAC device to express himself.

While the other students were limited to pushing buttons on their devices, he was spontaneously signing.

- He could tell me about his day, his favorite foods, and how he was feeling.
- He could share his love for football and debate which team was the best.
- He even shared his faith journey with me—something that would have been impossible on an AAC device, where conversations are often limited to basic wants and needs.

He wasn't just communicating—he was engaging, thinking, expressing emotions, and connecting. And here's the most powerful part: The other students saw this. They watched him communicate freely and started to realize that maybe, just maybe, they could do it too.

As the weeks went on, I noticed the other students watching me sign. Some of them started mimicking the signs, even though they were never formally introduced to ASL.

It started small. One student attempted the sign for "more" instead of pressing a button on their AAC device. Another student copied the sign for "help" after seeing me use it with the Deaf student.

By mid-year, I was teaching not just the students, but the paraprofessionals, teachers, and therapists in the classroom.

By the end of the year?

- Students who had never spoken a word were now using signs alongside their AAC devices.
- Paraprofessionals were reinforcing signs throughout the day.
- The classroom had transformed into a signing-inclusive space.

And it all started because of one Deaf student who had full access to language.

Why Isn't This the Standard for Special Education?

I remember walking out of that classroom thinking: Why isn't this the norm? Why do special educators go through their entire teacher training without a proper introduction to sign language? Why is ASL not included in every special education program, when we know that many neurodiverse children struggle with speech and need alternative communication methods?

AAC devices are widely accepted in special education. Why not sign language, too?

Sign language should not be seen as the last resort—it should be one of the first tools introduced to children with communication challenges.
This is why I started Signing Courses.

- To ensure that educators are properly trained in sign language so that no child is left without a way to communicate.
- To teach parents, teachers, and therapists that ASL is an accessible and powerful tool—not just for Deaf children, but for all children who struggle with speech.
- To bridge the gap in special education training, so that no teacher ever has to wonder how to help a child express themselves.

Because language access should never be an afterthought. Every child deserves a way to communicate—and sign language removes barriers that technology alone cannot. If we want to create truly inclusive classrooms, we need to start with language access. That's why I'm here. That's why our proprietary method exists.

Chapter 5: How Special Educators and Early Educators Can Use Signing Courses Flashcards and Posters from Day One

In this chapter, you will learn:

- Why sign language is an essential tool for special educators and early educators
- How to use Signing Courses Flashcards and Posters to create a language-rich classroom
- How to introduce signing from day one to establish consistency and engagement
- How to integrate sign language into classroom routines, transitions, and behavior management
- Ways to use ASL to support speech development, literacy, and subject-specific instruction
- How to train paraprofessionals, support staff, and parents in basic ASL for classroom success
- How schools and districts can book professional development training through Signing Courses

This chapter provides practical, hands-on strategies for using Signing Courses materials to ensure that sign language is effectively incorporated into your classroom from the very first day.

"Every person, Deaf or hearing, has a voice that matters." Marlee Matlin (Deaf Actress, Activist, and Academy Award Winner)

Special educators often work with students who have speech delays, neurodiverse conditions, or cognitive impairments that make verbal communication challenging. While many classrooms incorporate AAC devices, picture communication systems, or verbal prompting, sign language provides an additional, fully accessible tool that allows children to communicate more spontaneously and independently.

The Signing Courses Flashcards and Posters are specifically designed to help educators:

- Introduce ASL from the very first day of school
- Create a language-rich, inclusive classroom
- Support communication for both verbal and nonverbal students
- Reduce frustration and behavioral challenges by providing alternative ways to express needs

---

1. Setting Up a Signing-Inclusive Classroom from Day One

When students enter a special education classroom, they need clear communication tools that work for them. By incorporating ASL posters and flashcards into the environment immediately, educators establish signing as a natural part of the classroom routine.

How to Use Signing Courses Posters:

- Display core vocabulary posters in high-traffic areas such as the circle time area, near the whiteboard, and on the classroom door.
- Label stations with ASL signs, such as:
    - "Bathroom" – Posted near the restroom door
    - "Eat" and "Drink" – Displayed in the snack area
    - "Help" – Near student desks or learning stations
    - "Play" and "Wait" – In transition areas

By having consistent visual reinforcement of signs, students will begin associating words with their corresponding signs naturally.

How to Use Flashcards for Individual and Group Learning:

- Introduce a "Sign of the Day" by pulling a card each morning and teaching students how to use it in context.

- Use flashcards in small group instruction for matching games, role-playing, and visual reinforcement of new words.
- Send a flashcard home each week for families to practice together, ensuring that students receive reinforcement outside of the classroom.

---

2. Using Signs to Support Transitions and Behavior Management

For many neurodiverse students, verbal-only instructions can be overwhelming. Sign language provides a visual, predictable cue that helps students process directions more easily.

How to Use ASL for Transitions:

- Teach the sign for "wait" and use it consistently during transitions to help students self-regulate.
- Use the "sit" sign during circle time to reinforce expectations visually.
- Pair signs with auditory cues (e.g., signing "clean up" while playing the cleanup song).

By using signs alongside spoken words, educators reduce sensory overload and help students process directions in multiple ways.

How to Use ASL for Behavior Management:

- Instead of verbal redirections, use the "wait" sign to indicate when a behavior needs to pause.
- Teach self-regulation signs like "relax" or how to count to 10 in ASL for students who experience anxiety or frustration.
- Acknowledge positive behavior by signing "thank you" to provide nonverbal reinforcement.

---

3. Using ASL to Support AAC Device Users

While AAC devices are valuable tools, they often have limitations—they require programming, are dependent on battery life, and limit spontaneous communication.

Sign language can be used alongside AAC devices to provide additional communication support.

How to Use ASL with AAC Devices:

- Model signs as the child selects words on their device (e.g., when a student presses "help" on their AAC, the teacher also signs "help").
- Encourage students to pair signs with their AAC use, allowing them to develop motor memory for words.
- Use flashcards to reinforce AAC vocabulary, making communication more dynamic.

Many students who start with AAC eventually transition to using signs for faster, more natural communication.

---

4. Incorporating Signs into Academic Instruction

Sign language is not just for behavior management and communication—it can also enhance literacy, math, and subject-specific instruction.

Using ASL for Literacy Development:

- Pair signs with sight words using Signing Courses flashcards to help students memorize words faster.
- Use finger spelling to reinforce letter recognition and spelling practice.
- Sign key vocabulary words during read-alouds to engage students and strengthen comprehension.

Using ASL for Math Instruction:

- Teach students to sign numbers as they count to reinforce number recognition.
- Use signs for addition, subtraction, and more/less to help students visualize math concepts.

Using ASL in Science & Social Studies:

- Use Signing Courses Posters to introduce key vocabulary words for science topics (e.g., weather, animals, health).
- Teach emotion and history-related signs when discussing social-emotional learning and cultural studies.

By making signing part of academic instruction, educators ensure that students with communication delays are actively engaged in all subjects.

5. Teaching Paraprofessionals and Classroom Support Staff to Sign

Special education classrooms often have multiple paraprofessionals, therapists, and support staff who work with students daily. To create a truly inclusive communication environment, it's important that everyone knows basic signs.

How to Train Staff Using Signing Courses Materials:

- Hold a weekly "Sign Training" session using Signing Courses flashcards.
- Post ASL reference charts in staff break areas to encourage learning.
- Pair staff members with students who use ASL so they can practice during one-on-one time.

By ensuring that all staff members are familiar with basic signs, educators create a consistent, language-rich classroom where students always have a way to communicate.

Booking Signing Courses for Professional Development

Most special educators do not receive proper training in sign language during their teacher preparation programs. Many graduate without ever learning how to incorporate ASL into their classrooms, even though millions of children struggle with speech and language delays.

This is why Signing Courses offers professional development training—to fill that gap and ensure that all educators have the tools they need to make their classrooms more accessible and inclusive.

Why Schools Should Book a Signing Courses Professional Development Session:

- Educators will learn practical ASL strategies that they can implement immediately.
- Teachers and staff will receive hands-on training using Signing Courses flashcards and posters.
- Schools will create a more inclusive learning environment, benefiting both verbal and nonverbal students.

- Participants will leave with a clear plan for using sign language effectively in their classrooms.

How to Book a Session:

- Schools, districts, and individual educators can book a professional development session through the Signing Courses website.
- Virtual and in-person training options are available.
- Sessions are customized to meet the specific needs of each school or classroom.

The 4-Year-Old Who Found Her Voice Through Signing

One afternoon, I got a phone call from an early educator who sounded both excited and overwhelmed. She had a four-year-old student in her classroom who would not use speech, no matter what strategies they tried. The child had been in the program for months, but she never spoke—not a single word.

The teacher was desperate for a new approach. She wanted to help the child communicate but wasn't sure what to do. I immediately knew that signing could be the missing piece.

I provided her with the Signing Courses Flashcards and Posters and walked her through how to introduce signs using The Signing Courses Method. I told her:

1. Hang the posters around the classroom so the signs were always visible.
2. Choose a few essential signs to start with—like more, help, eat, all done, and wait—and model them consistently.
3. Encourage but never force signing, allowing the child to observe and learn naturally.
4. Make signing part of daily routines—using signs during mealtimes, transitions, and activities.
5. Teach everyone in the classroom (teachers, paraprofessionals, and other students) to ensure a signing-rich environment.

She followed the plan, implementing the Signing Courses Method with full commitment.

By week four, the child was signing—and speaking. For the first time, she was expressing

her needs, participating in class, and engaging
with her peers. She signed "help" when she needed assistance. She signed "more" and then spoke the word aloud.

When the child's parents saw what was happening, they cried. They had waited four

years to hear their child's voice, and now she was signing and speaking because she was finally given a way to communicate without pressure or frustration.

This moment wasn't just about learning a few signs—it was about unlocking a child's

ability to communicate, connect, and feel understood.
The teacher told me later that signing transformed her classroom, not just for that one

child but for all her students. More children began using signs alongside speech, and the overall classroom environment became calmer, more inclusive, and more engaging. And all it took was one set of flashcards, one set of posters, and a structured method that actually works– and an educator who was willing to try something new.

Chapter 6: The Deaf Community's Gift to Language Development

Sign language exists because of the Deaf community. It is not a collection of gestures or an alternative form of spoken language—it is a fully developed, complex language with its own grammar, syntax, and linguistic structure. ASL was not created for hearing children to use as a temporary tool—it has existed for generations as the primary language of Deaf people.

Because of this, it is essential to honor the Deaf community when teaching and using sign language. We learn in this chapter that we must:

- Use real ASL instead of "made-up" signs.
- Understand the history of Deaf culture and language suppression.
- Advocate for ASL as a valid language for all children.

When we embrace signing, we do more than give children a way to communicate—we celebrate, preserve, and respect the rich culture and history of the Deaf community.

"The best and most beautiful things in the world cannot be seen or even touched—they must be felt with the heart." Helen Keller (Deaf-Blind Author & Activist)

The Deaf Community: The Reason ASL Exists

Sign language was not invented by educators or speech therapists—it came from Deaf people themselves. Deaf individuals have always found ways to communicate, and for centuries, they have created, expanded, and passed down their own languages.

American Sign Language (ASL) originated from Deaf people teaching each other, combining regional sign variations and influences from French Sign Language (LSF) to develop a unique, standardized language. It has since evolved into a rich, expressive, and dynamic language that continues to grow today.

The Deaf community's contributions to language development go beyond just ASL. Deaf individuals have pioneered advancements in bilingual education, visual learning strategies, and linguistic research, proving that language does not require sound to be powerful, meaningful, and effective.

When we teach sign language, we are using a language that belongs to the Deaf community—and that comes with the responsibility to respect, preserve, and advocate for it.

Using Real ASL Instead of "Made-Up" Signs

Many educators, speech therapists, and caregivers unknowingly create "home signs" or made-up gestures instead of using real ASL. While these gestures may serve a temporary purpose, they are not a language and do not provide children with a foundation for long-term communication.

- ASL has a structured linguistic system—random gestures do not.
- Made-up signs isolate children from the larger Deaf community.
- Using ASL ensures children have access to a legitimate, recognized language that they can continue using for life.

By using real ASL signs, children are being taught a language that has depth, history, and real-world applications. They are also being given the ability to connect with the Deaf community if they choose to later in life.

A parent or teacher might create a gesture for "water" by mimicking the motion of drinking from an invisible cup instead of using the actual ASL sign for "water" (a "W" handshape tapping the chin).

While this made-up gesture may work at home or in the classroom, what happens when the child tries to communicate with a Deaf individual?

- The Deaf person will not recognize the gesture because it is not an ASL sign.
- The child will need to relearn the correct ASL sign later, making the process more difficult.
- The child misses the opportunity to communicate with the broader signing community.

Rather than using temporary solutions, it is crucial to provide children with real, lasting language access.

That said, in some classroom settings, educators may choose to use the sign for "drink" instead of "water" to prompt communication, as it may be easier for a child to produce. This is acceptable as long as the educator understands the distinction and is prepared to shift toward ASL-specific signs when needed—for example, if a Deaf child enters the classroom.

Being aware of these differences allows educators to create a communication-rich environment that supports all learners while remaining respectful of ASL as a complete and structured language.

The History of Deaf Culture and Language Suppression

To fully understand why we must respect ASL, we need to acknowledge the history of language suppression in the Deaf community.

For centuries, Deaf people have fought for the right to use their own language. ASL was once banned in schools, and Deaf children were forced to learn through oralism—a method that focused on lip-reading and speech production while prohibiting sign language.

- Deaf children were punished for signing in classrooms.
- Many Deaf individuals were denied education and job opportunities if they did not speak.
- Entire generations of Deaf people were linguistically oppressed and forced to communicate in ways that did not fully serve them.

Despite these obstacles, the Deaf community persevered. ASL was passed down in Deaf schools, homes, and social gatherings, and eventually, linguistic research proved what Deaf people had always known—sign language is a fully developed, natural language.

Today, ASL is recognized as a legitimate language in education, research, and public policy, but the fight for language access is not over. Many hearing educators, speech therapists, and schools still push oralism over signing, despite overwhelming evidence that sign language benefits all children, whether Deaf, hard of hearing, or hearing.

By choosing to use ASL in early education, we are actively undoing the harm of language suppression and ensuring that sign language is valued, respected, and preserved.

Why We Must Advocate for ASL as a Valid Language for All Children

Sign language is not just for Deaf children—it is a valuable language for all children. However, many parents and educators are still hesitant to introduce ASL because they believe spoken language is superior.

This mindset is rooted in historical biases against sign language, which continue to impact Deaf education today. Many Deaf children are still denied access to ASL in favor of spoken language approaches, despite research showing that bilingual ASL-English education leads to better outcomes for Deaf children.

ASL Should Be Taught Alongside Speech

1. ASL is a full, expressive language—not just a tool for children who can't speak yet.
2. Learning sign language does not prevent speech development—in fact, it can enhance it.
3. Children who learn ASL early develop stronger communication skills, even if they go on to speak fluently.
4. ASL provides language access for children with speech delays, autism, and other communication challenges.

We should be advocating for ASL as a first language option, rather than treating it as a backup plan. If more educators were trained in ASL, fewer children would experience language deprivation—a completely preventable crisis that continues to affect Deaf children today.

Honoring the Deaf Community in Early Education

If we are teaching sign language in our classrooms, we must do so with respect for the Deaf community.

- Acknowledge that ASL comes from the Deaf community—it is not just a tool for hearing children.
- Use accurate ASL signs instead of gestures or made-up signs.
- Teach about Deaf culture, history, and the importance of language accessibility.
- Advocate for ASL to be included in early education and special education programs.
- Encourage families to expose children to Deaf culture, events, and sign language resources.

When we introduce sign language in our classrooms, we should be celebrating and respecting the community that created it. Sign language is a gift. That gift comes from the Deaf community. It is our responsibility to honor that gift, use it correctly, and advocate for its rightful place in education.

Finding Connection in the Deaf Community

When I was in college, I wanted to immerse myself in ASL beyond the classroom. Learning sign language from books and lectures was great, but I knew that true fluency came from real-life experiences—from being in Deaf spaces, signing with Deaf people, and embracing the culture firsthand.

That's when I found the Deaf Club in Ohio.

Every week, I would go to the club, a gathering space where Deaf people would come together to socialize, play games, and just be in a space where ASL was the dominant language. No interpreters, no need for speech—just signing, community, and belonging. One of my favorite nights was DINGO night—Deaf Bingo.

DINGO was just like regular bingo, but entirely in ASL. The numbers would be signed, the jokes were signed, the conversations during breaks were signed—it was full immersion. There was no way to sit there quietly or rely on spoken language. If you wanted to engage, you had to sign.

At first, I felt intimidated. Everyone around me was signing so fast. I struggled to keep up with the jokes and catch every sign, even though I grew up in the Deaf community. But the Deaf community is welcoming—as long as you genuinely want to learn and respect the language, they will meet you where you are.

The more I showed up, the more comfortable I became. I started recognizing regional signs that weren't in my textbooks or from my hometown. I learned how to hold full conversations without hesitation. My fingers became quicker, my comprehension sharper, my confidence stronger.

The Deaf Club wasn't just a place to practice ASL—it was a place to build friendships, cultural understanding, and true language immersion.

Why Every ASL Learner Should Find a Deaf Community

If you truly want to learn ASL, not just simple signing, you need to go where ASL is naturally used.

You can start with the ASL book my father and I co-authored, ***Barron's American Sign Language: A Comprehensive Guide to ASL 1 and 2, David A. Stewart Ed.D. (Author)***, *Jennifer Stewart M.S.Ed.(Author).*   However, most classrooms and apps can teach vocabulary and conversational sign language, but only Deaf spaces can teach you how to truly communicate.

- Deaf events, Deaf coffee nights, and Deaf clubs are where you will see real conversational ASL—not just structured lessons.
- You will pick up expressions, body language, and cultural norms that you can't learn from a book.

- You will develop deeper connections and a true appreciation for Deaf culture and history.

I always tell my students, "If you want to be fluent in ASL, go where ASL is the primary language. Find a Deaf club. Go to a Deaf event. Put yourself in a space where signing is your only option." That is where your skills will grow the most.

For me, the Deaf Club in Ohio was more than just a place to learn—it was a place where I built relationships, gained confidence, and became part of a community that welcomed me because I respected their language and culture. If you truly want to learn ASL, find a place like that. Go, sign, learn, and immerse yourself. It will change everything.

Chapter 7: Growing Up as a CODA

Growing up as a CODA (Child of a Deaf Adult) means having a life full of bilingual, bicultural moments—some funny, some profound, and some that, at the time, felt completely normal until I realized that most families don't communicate via fax or have sideline coaching in ASL.

Deaf culture is unique in so many ways, and I was lucky to grow up immersed in it. But looking back, some of my favorite moments weren't just about language—they were about how Deaf culture operates differently from the hearing world, and how, as a CODA, I got to experience both sides.

In this chapter we learn about these unique cultural experiences and how I use what I have learned to teach others.

_____

"It is not the eyes or the ears that bring a person knowledge, but the mind." Laurent Clerc (Deaf Educator, Co-Founder of the First School for the Deaf in America)

The Deaf Wave – The Proper Way to Get a Deaf Person's Attention

People always ask, "What's the right way to get a Deaf person's attention?" and my answer is simple:

You use the Deaf Wave.

It's not dramatic. It's not over-the-top. It's a low flutter of the fingers, just enough to say, "Hey, I'm here!" It's classy, effective, and most importantly—it doesn't involve yelling.

Because let's be real: why would you yell? There are also other ways to get a Deaf person's attention. Flickering the lights is a good one, but please, not like you're trying to start a rave—just a simple, respectful flash. My dad? He had this down to a science.

When he was napping—hearing aids off, completely in his own quiet world—we needed a way to let him know when it was dinnertime. Did we stomp down the stairs? Nope. Did we yell? Absolutely not. We flickered the lights. And like magic—boom. He'd be up and ready to eat.

Looking back, I laugh at how efficient and peaceful it was compared to the chaos of yelling across the house like many hearing families do. In the Deaf world, light flickers are the universal dinner bell.

And yes, kid-me definitely abused this power sometimes. *Flicker flicker—Dad, I need you!* No reason, just felt like summoning him like a wizard. But really, it's a perfect example of Deaf culture in action—finding simple, effective, non-verbal ways to communicate.

Deaf People Were the Original Texters: Life Before Smartphones

People think text messaging is a modern invention. Nope. Deaf people were doing it first.

Back in the day, before we had iPhones, FaceTime, or instant messaging, my dad had a TTY (teletypewriter). This glorious, clunky machine let Deaf people type messages back and forth over the phone.

- Type your message.
- Wait for the other person to type back.
- Read their response.
- Repeat.

It was like texting at the speed of a typewriter, and if you wanted to talk to a hearing person, you had to go through a relay operator, who would read your typed messages out loud to the hearing caller and then type their response back.

Imagine how awkward some of these conversations got.

Example:

- My dad types: "Hello, I need to confirm my hotel reservation for David Stewart."
- The relay operator reads it to the hotel clerk.
- The hotel clerk, confused: "Wait… who am I talking to?"
- The relay operator: "This is a relay service. The caller is Deaf. Please continue speaking, and I will type your responses."
- Hotel clerk, still panicking: "Oh, … okay?"

This was the reality of Deaf communication before smartphones.

Fax Machine Conversations: Long-Distance Deaf Communication, 90s Style

Yes, you read that right. We used to communicate via fax.

Here's how it worked:

1. My dad would call home from a hotel phone and say, "Hey! How's everything going?"
2. Since he couldn't hear our response, we would yell, "WE'RE GOOD!" …which, obviously, he couldn't hear.
3. So instead, we'd write down our response on a piece of paper, load it into the fax machine, and fax it to his hotel.
4. A few minutes later, the fax machine would ring again—his reply had arrived.

That's right—we were texting before texting was a thing, just at the speed of a fax machine.

Looking back, I find it hilarious that faxing was how we had family conversations, but at the time, it was just how Deaf-hearing communication worked in a pre-smartphone world.

Sideline Coaching in ASL – A Soccer Advantage

Now, let's talk about soccer. While most parents screamed from the sidelines, my dad had an advantage—sign language.

Signing is faster than yelling because:

1. It's visual. No waiting for your kid to hear you over the crowd noise.
2. It's immediate. No lag time, just pure instant communication.

3. It's a secret. The other team has no idea what you're saying.

So while my teammates' parents were shouting vague instructions, my dad was signing exactly what I needed to do.

1. "MOVE LEFT!" (Quick ASL sign for "left" + intense pointing.)

2. "LOOK AT THE BALL!" (Eye sign + ball sign + big exaggerated gestures.)

3. "SCORE!" (Super clear sign for "put the ball in the goal, already".)

And let's not forget the Deaf dad celebrations. My dad had a strong speaking voice, but since he couldn't hear himself, his cheering came out in full, unapologetic CODA-approved volume along with applause.

Meanwhile, my teammates would ask, "What did your dad just say?" Me: *"Uh… he signed 'GOOD JOB!'"*

They had no idea I was getting private, high-speed coaching in real-time, while they had to wait for their parents' voices to reach them. CODA advantage unlocked.

What's In a Name? The Cultural Acceptance of a Name-Sign.

In Deaf culture, name-signs hold deep significance and are not something you can create for yourself. A true name-sign can only be given by a Deaf individual and is typically based on a person's physical features, personality traits, or unique habits. This tradition is an important part of Deaf identity and community acceptance. When I received my name sign, it originally started with a "J" handshape since my name begins with "J." However, as time went on, it evolved into an "R" handshape twisting down from my hair—because I have a habit of twirling my hair. This was a natural way for the Deaf people around me to identify me in a way that was both personal and visually descriptive.

While name-signs carry cultural significance, there are times—such as in classrooms—when educators or students may create a temporary "sign-name or name-sign" for ease of communication. In educational settings, it can be beneficial for teachers to assign themselves a quick and functional name sign so that children, especially those who are Deaf or nonverbal, have a way to refer to them. These signs are often based on the first letter of the person's name combined with a distinguishing characteristic. For example, a teacher named "Ms. Sarah" might use an "S" handshape tapping the shoulder. However, it's important to remember that these classroom name signs are not culturally recognized name signs and should not be mistaken for one given by the Deaf community.

When using name signs in a classroom, it's a great opportunity to teach students about Deaf culture and respect for its traditions. Children can have fun assigning each other signs based on visual traits or interests, but they should also learn that official name signs come from Deaf individuals and are a mark of community acceptance. By introducing this cultural concept with respect, educators can help children understand the importance of ASL traditions while making signing a natural part of the learning environment. If a Deaf student or teacher is present, they might even choose to give official name signs to students or staff, further deepening the connection between the classroom and the Deaf community.

Growing up, I thought all kids had fax conversations with their parents, TTY machines in their houses, and parents who coached them from the sidelines in ASL. I didn't realize I was bicultural and bilingual—I just thought this was how life worked.

- ASL was my first language.

- Deaf culture was my normal.

- I existed in two worlds at once without even realizing it.

It wasn't until I got older—when I started studying ASL interpreting and working with Deaf students—that I fully understood the uniqueness of being a CODA. I wasn't just someone who learned ASL—I lived it, breathed it, and carried it with me in everything I did.

And now, as I teach others, I carry my father's legacy forward—through sign language, through education, and through the shared stories of what it truly means to grow up as a CODA in a Deaf-hearing world.

Chapter 8: A Guide for Educators – Teaching Deaf and Hard-of-Hearing Students

Teaching a Deaf or hard-of-hearing (DHH) student is not simply about accommodating hearing loss—it is about ensuring full language access, inclusion, and equal educational opportunities. Deaf children are not broken, nor do they need to be "fixed" with hearing aids or cochlear implants alone. They need a complete language from day one and a classroom that supports their linguistic and cultural needs.

This chapter will provide educators with;

- Essential knowledge and strategies to create a successful, accessible, and inclusive learning environment for Deaf and hard-of-hearing students.

"Deaf people can do anything hearing people can do, except hear." King Jordan (First Deaf President of Gallaudet University)

What Every Educator Needs to Know About Deaf Students

If you have a Deaf or hard-of-hearing child in your class, here's what you need to know:

- ASL is their first language – treat it with the same respect as English.
- They need full language access – visual supports and sign language are essential.
- Deaf children should not be isolated – create an inclusive environment.

Deaf students thrive when their language needs are met, their identity is respected, and their education is fully accessible. Too often, however, Deaf students are placed in classrooms where they are expected to adapt to hearing environments instead of having the environment adapt to them.

Many schools still prioritize speech over signing, even when research shows that bilingual education (ASL and English) leads to the best outcomes for Deaf students.

If we want to truly support Deaf students, we must do more than accommodate—we must empower them with the tools, language, and learning environment they need to succeed.

ASL Is Their First Language – Treat It with the Same Respect as English

Many Deaf children grow up in homes where spoken language is inaccessible. If they do not have signing family members, school becomes the first place where they have full access to language.

As an educator, it is crucial to:

- Recognize ASL as a complete, legitimate language with its own grammar and structure.
- Ensure Deaf students have full access to their first language in the classroom.
- Avoid treating ASL as an "extra tool" or "accommodation"—it is their primary mode of communication.

The most successful approach to Deaf education is bilingual education, where Deaf students learn in both ASL and English.

- ASL provides full language access for learning concepts.
- English is introduced through print and reading instruction.
- Deaf students learn to read and write in English while using ASL as their primary language.

A bilingual approach removes language barriers and ensures that Deaf children are developing literacy skills without being forced into a spoken language that may not be fully accessible to them.

- Provide classroom materials in both ASL and English (e.g., ASL videos alongside written text).
- Use ASL for instruction whenever possible, rather than relying solely on spoken English with captions.
- Ensure Deaf students have Deaf role models, whether through teachers, guest speakers, or video content.

A Deaf student in an ASL-rich environment will thrive academically, socially, and emotionally because they will have access to a full and complete language.

They Need Full Language Access – Visual Supports and Sign Language Are Essential

Deaf students learn visually. They rely on sight, movement, and spatial awareness to process information. If an educator only provides spoken instruction, even with assistive devices like hearing aids or FM systems, the Deaf student will miss significant portions of the lesson.

How to Provide Full Language Access in the Classroom

- Use ASL fluently if you know it—or have an ASL interpreter present for full communication access. This is not an option, this is the law. The Americans with Disabilities Act ensures an ASL Interpreter can and will be hired for any and all Deaf students.
- Make sure the Deaf student has a clear line of sight to the teacher, interpreter, and board.
- Use visual supports like written instructions, pictures, videos with captions, and hands-on demonstrations.
- Face the student when speaking and avoid talking while writing on the board.
- Incorporate technology, such as captioned educational videos, ASL storytelling apps, and visual learning tools.

When language access is incomplete, a Deaf student falls behind—not because they lack intelligence, but because they are not receiving the full message . A Deaf student should never have to struggle to understand their education. It is the educator's responsibility to ensure full accessibility in every lesson.

Lip reading, often assumed to be an effective communication tool for Deaf individuals, is highly unreliable and ineffective as a sole means of understanding spoken language. While many hearing people believe that Deaf individuals can "just read lips," the reality is that only about 30% of English sounds are visible on the lips, leaving the remaining 70% of speech completely ambiguous. Certain sounds, like "p" and "b" or "f" and "v," look nearly identical on the lips, making it impossible to distinguish between words without additional context. Furthermore, many sounds are produced inside the mouth and throat, making them invisible to the eye, which causes major gaps in comprehension.

Even in ideal conditions—where the speaker is facing the Deaf individual, speaking clearly, and in good lighting—lip reading is still guesswork at best. The English language is full of homophones, meaning that multiple words can look identical on the lips but have completely different meanings. For example, "mom" and "bob" or "pat" and "bat" appear the same, forcing a Deaf person to rely heavily on context and facial expressions to piece together meaning. Add in accents, mustaches, beards, fast speech, or mumbling, and the ability to read lips becomes even more difficult. The mental effort required to fill in the blanks and guess words leads to fatigue and frustration, making lip reading an exhausting and often ineffective communication method.

Relying on lip reading as a primary means of communication excludes Deaf individuals from full language access and often results in misunderstandings and incomplete information. This is why sign language is critical—it provides full, direct, and accessible communication that does not rely on guessing or partial comprehension. Instead of expecting Deaf individuals to struggle through reading only a fraction of spoken language, it is far more inclusive to use ASL, captions, or written text to ensure complete understanding. Communication should be about accessibility, not making Deaf people work harder to fit into a hearing-centric world.

Deaf Children Should Not Be Isolated

Too often, Deaf students are placed in classrooms where they are the only Deaf person, leaving them feeling isolated and disconnected. Many Deaf students are:

- Left out of group discussions because they cannot follow fast-paced spoken conversations.
- Excluded from social activities because their peers do not sign.
- Treated as an "exception" instead of as an equal member of the class.

This isolation can have a significant impact on self-esteem, academic motivation, and social development.

How to Create an Inclusive Classroom for Deaf Students

- Encourage all students to learn basic ASL so the Deaf student can interact with peers.
- Assign peer buddies who can communicate with the Deaf student.
- Use inclusive teaching methods that do not rely solely on spoken language.
- Advocate for more Deaf representation in school events, activities, and leadership roles.
- Create a Deaf-friendly classroom culture, where ASL is respected and valued.

An inclusive classroom benefits all students—not just the Deaf student. When ASL is included in the curriculum, hearing students gain a second language, better communication skills, and a greater appreciation for diversity.

Learning from My Deaf Father's Words

This chapter pulls directly from the teachings and writings of David Stewart, my father—a trailblazing Deaf educator, researcher, and author. He spent his career teaching thousands of Deaf students and writing the book on how to do it—literally. His book, *Teaching Deaf and Hard of Hearing Children*, has shaped the way educators approach Deaf education, ensuring that Deaf students receive the language access, inclusion, and respect they deserve.

It is surreal to now be writing a chapter that draws from his work—because for me, his teachings were never just words in a book. They were my childhood, my foundation, my everyday life.

When I decided to pursue my Master's in Special Education and earn my Teaching Deaf Children certification, I expected to learn from respected experts in the field. But nothing could have prepared me for the moment when I opened my course syllabus and saw my father's name on the required reading list.

His book, *Teaching Deaf and Hard of Hearing Children*, was listed as one of the foundational texts for my degree.

The university required us to buy a copy, but of course—I already had one. I had read it before. I had lived it before. I had learned these lessons not just from the pages but from growing up watching my father teach Deaf students with passion, commitment, and deep cultural understanding. He used the same teaching methods with his four hearing children.

I didn't tell anyone in my program that my father was the David Stewart listed on our reading list. I quietly went along with the class discussions, absorbing everything as if I were learning it for the first time—even though, in reality, these lessons had been ingrained in me since childhood.

Every chapter, every theory, every strategy—I had seen it firsthand in my father's classroom, in his work, in his advocacy for Deaf students.

Before becoming a teacher of Deaf students, I was an ASL interpreter. And just like with Deaf education, I found myself learning from my father's work again—this time through his book on ASL interpreting.

His research and writings shaped how I approached interpreting, reinforcing that interpreters are not just there to sign words—they are language facilitators, cultural mediators, and advocates for communication access.

Then came another moment that made me realize just how far-reaching my father's impact was.

One day, I was sitting in the dean's office in my ASL interpreting program, waiting for a meeting. I glanced over at her desk and there, sitting right on top of a stack of books, was one of my father's ASL interpreting books. I couldn't help myself—I casually pointed to it and said, "My dad wrote that." The dean's head snapped up, looking at me in surprise. "Your dad is David Stewart?" she asked.

That was the moment that everyone in my ASL interpreting program learned I was a CODA (Child of Deaf Adult). Until then, I had just been another interpreting student. No one knew that my entire life had been shaped by Deaf culture, by ASL, by a father whose teachings were now sitting in front of them on a desk.

That day, I realized that my father's work had reached places far beyond our home, beyond his classroom, beyond what I had even imagined.

Now, as I write this book—pulling from my own experiences and my father's teachings—I see how his work continues through mine.

- The lessons he taught his Deaf students are the same lessons I teach today.
- The research he conducted on Deaf education informs how I train educators.
- The books he wrote are the same books that helped shape me into the educator, interpreter, and advocate I am today.

And now, as I teach others through Signing Courses, I feel that same responsibility—to ensure that Deaf students have access to full language, full inclusion, and full respect in the classroom. Because that is the legacy my father left, and it's one I will always continue.

Chapter 9: Common Myths About Sign Language Debunked

Sign language is backed by decades of scientific research proving its benefits for all children.

When people challenge the value of ASL, remind them that:

- Signing enhances speech, not delays it—but only when introduced properly.
- All children—not just Deaf children—benefit from sign language.
- Signing is not difficult to learn—you only need a few essential signs.
- Children with disabilities can learn to sign and benefit from it.
- You don't need to be fluent in ASL—The Signing Courses Method provides exactly what you need.

By debunking these myths with science and real-world evidence, we can ensure that more children gain access to the benefits of signing—without outdated misconceptions getting in the way.

"Deaf people have unique experiences and perspectives that contribute to the richness of the world." Thomas Gallaudet (Pioneer of Deaf Education in America)

Even with decades of research proving the benefits of sign language, misconceptions persist. Educators, parents, and even medical professionals often misunderstand the role of ASL, leading to missed opportunities for language access. We have touched on a few of these misconceptions, but now let's go into what we can say when confronted with them in real-time.

Myth #1: "Signing will delay speech."

False! Research shows signing enhances verbal skills.

What to Say:
 "Actually, research proves that signing helps children develop speech faster, not slower. Babies and toddlers who sign tend to have larger vocabularies and stronger language skills than those who don't."

The Evidence:

- A study by Dr. Linda Acredolo and Dr. Susan Goodwyn (2000) found that babies who used sign language had larger spoken vocabularies by age two than non-signing babies.
- Research in neurolinguistics shows that signing activates the same brain areas as spoken language, reinforcing verbal development rather than replacing it.
- The National Institute on Deafness and Other Communication Disorders (NIDCD) states that signing does not delay speech but rather provides a bridge to verbal communication.

However, if sign language is not introduced correctly, it can cause delays in speech development.

If you do not use The Signing Courses Method, you may actually delay speech because:

- Signs must be introduced consistently and in context for children to connect them with spoken words.
- If signs are not paired with verbal speech, children may not develop strong verbal associations.
- If caregivers fail to model signs frequently, children will not get enough exposure to develop language fluency.

Key Takeaway:

Signing enhances language learning when introduced correctly. The Signing Courses Method ensures that signing supports verbal language instead of replacing it.

Myth #2: "Only Deaf children need sign language."

False! All children benefit from ASL.

What to Say:

"Sign language is for everyone, not just Deaf children. Research shows that signing improves communication, reduces frustration, and enhances cognitive development in both hearing and non-hearing children."

The Evidence:

- The American Speech-Language-Hearing Association (ASHA) confirms that sign language is a valuable tool for all children, especially those with speech delays, autism, or other communication disorders.
- Studies show that bilingual children (including those learning ASL and English) develop stronger executive function skills, such as problem-solving and memory retention.
- AAC research supports sign language as an effective form of communication for children with speech and language disorders, helping them express themselves before verbal language develops.

Key Takeaway:

Sign language is a universal tool that benefits all children, regardless of hearing status. It is particularly effective for bilingual learners, children with speech delays, and neurodiverse learners.

Myth #3: "Signing is too hard to learn."

False! You can start with just a few simple signs.

What to Say:

"Learning sign language is no harder than learning spoken words. In fact, children naturally pick up signs as easily as they do gestures like waving or pointing."

The Evidence:

- Studies on early childhood development show that babies as young as six months can recognize and use simple signs before they are able to speak.
- Research in motor learning indicates that signing is often easier for young children than forming spoken words because fine motor skills develop before verbal articulation.
- The Signing Courses Method has successfully helped thousands of children learn ASL with just a few basic signs to start (e.g., "more," "eat," "help").

Key Takeaway:

You don't need to be fluent in ASL to start signing with children. A few key signs can make an immediate difference in communication and language development.

Myth #4: "Children with disabilities can't learn signs."

False! Sign language is one of the best tools for children with disabilities.

What to Say:

"Sign language is accessible for all children, including those with autism, Down syndrome, apraxia, and cognitive delays. Many children with disabilities find signing easier than speaking because it removes the pressure of verbal articulation."

The Evidence:

- The American Speech-Language-Hearing Association (ASHA) recognizes sign language as an effective AAC (Augmentative and Alternative Communication) strategy for children with speech delays.
- A study in the *Journal of Autism and Developmental Disorders* found that children with autism who used sign language experienced fewer communication-related behavioral outbursts than those who did not.
- Children with apraxia and other motor-planning difficulties benefit from ASL because signing requires fewer oral-motor movements than speech.

Key Takeaway:

Sign language is a lifeline for children with communication challenges. It is a multi-sensory approach that helps them express needs, emotions, and thoughts—even if they struggle with verbal speech.

Myth #5: "You have to learn all of ASL to use signs with children."

False! You only need to know the essential signs taught in The Signing Courses Method.

What to Say:

"You don't need to be fluent in ASL to start using signs with children. You only need a handful of key signs that fit into daily routines. The Signing Courses Method teaches you exactly what you need to know—without the pressure of learning the entire language."

The Evidence:

- Early childhood language studies show that children benefit from even minimal exposure to signing, as it reinforces verbal speech.
- Research in language acquisition indicates that starting with just 5-10 core signs can provide children with a functional communication system.
- The Signing Courses Method focuses on high-impact, daily-use signs that are immediately useful, such as:
    - More
    - Eat
    - Help
    - All done
    - Please

Key Takeaway:

You don't need to learn the entire ASL language to introduce signing. The Signing Courses Method makes it simple, effective, and accessible for educators, parents, and caregivers.

When discussing sign language with educators, parents, or professionals, you may encounter pushback, skepticism, or outdated misconceptions. While it's easy to become frustrated, especially when you know the scientific research and real-world success behind signing, it's more effective to approach these conversations with patience, understanding, and facts.

Here are some more in-depth, polite and professional ways to respond when someone presents these myths to you:

Myth #1: "Signing will delay speech."

What to Say Politely:

"I completely understand why you might think that! A lot of people have heard that myth, but actually, research shows that signing helps children develop speech faster. Babies who sign tend to have larger spoken vocabularies by age two. Signing provides a strong foundation for verbal communication, rather than replacing it."

Then, if appropriate, share a quick research fact:

"For example, a study by Dr. Linda Acredolo and Dr. Susan Goodwyn found that signing babies had stronger verbal skills than non-signing babies by age two. Signing actually supports language development rather than delaying it."

Myth #2: "Only Deaf children need sign language."

What to Say Politely:

"That's a really common belief! However, sign language is actually beneficial for all children, especially those who are still developing speech. Many neurodiverse children, bilingual learners, and children with speech delays use sign language as a bridge to spoken communication."

Offer a real-world example:

"In fact, many speech-language pathologists recommend signing for children with speech delays because it gives them a way to communicate while they're working on verbal skills. It's not just for Deaf children—it's a valuable tool for any child learning language."

Myth #3: "Signing is too hard to learn."

What to Say Politely:

"I used to think that too! But the good news is, you don't need to learn the entire

language to make a difference. Just a few simple signs like 'more,' 'help,' and 'all done' can have a huge impact on communication. You can start small and build from there!"

If they still seem hesitant, offer reassurance:
 "I actually teach an easy method that helps people start with just a handful of essential signs that fit into their daily routine. It's much easier than people think!"

Myth #4: "Children with disabilities can't learn signs."

What to Say Politely:
 "I completely understand that concern, but research actually shows that sign language is one of the best tools for children with disabilities. Many children with autism, Down syndrome, and speech delays find signing easier than speaking because it removes the pressure of verbal articulation."

Provide an example:
 "I worked with a child who had apraxia, and signing gave him a way to express himself while he was working on verbal speech. It reduced his frustration and actually helped improve his ability to communicate over time."

Myth #5: "You have to learn all of ASL to use signs with children."

What to Say Politely:
"That's a really common misconception! You don't need to be fluent in ASL to start using signs. In fact, I teach a method that focuses only on the most useful signs that help with daily communication. You can start with just a few and see immediate results!"

Encourage them to try it:
 "If you're interested, I can show you a couple of simple signs right now—it's really easy to start, and kids pick it up naturally!"

How to Handle Someone Who Still Isn't Convinced

If you've politely shared information and they still resist, don't argue or push. Instead, redirect the conversation by inviting them to explore it further:

- "I totally understand! If you ever want to see how signing works in action, I'd be happy to show you a quick demo."
- "There's actually a lot of research on this—if you're curious, I can send you some links to studies that show the benefits of signing."
- "I've seen signing make a huge difference for so many kids—if you ever want to try it, I'd love to help."

Sometimes, people need time to process new information. By remaining calm, professional, and encouraging, you keep the door open for future learning rather than shutting it down with confrontation.

Chapter 10: Practical Strategies for Classrooms and Home Environments – Connecting with Families and Bringing Everything Together

Introducing sign language into the classroom or home is not just about teaching children a few signs—it's about creating an inclusive environment where language access is natural, enjoyable, and fully supported. We have learned the basics about signing and Deaf culture, and now it is time to bring it all together.

For ASL to be successful in any educational setting, it must be embraced beyond the teacher and student dynamic—it must be supported by families, administrators, and educational policies. Sign language works best when it's woven into everyday interactions, backed by school-wide support, and included in formal education plans like 504 Plans or IEPs.

This chapter will;

- Provide practical strategies for integrating sign language seamlessly into both classroom and home environments while ensuring that families, administration, and program directors are on board.

"The lack of communication is the greatest barrier to success for Deaf people." Andrew Foster (First Black Deaf Educator and Founder of Deaf Schools in Africa)

The Role of Families in Supporting Sign Language Learning

One of the most common challenges in early and special education is a lack of family involvement in sign language learning. Many parents want to support their child's communication but don't know where to start. Others may feel intimidated by ASL or worry that they need to become fluent before using it at home.

- Send home ASL flashcards or printable sheets so parents can learn key signs.
- Encourage parents to attend ASL workshops or Deaf community events.
- Provide short instructional videos (Signing Courses has these!) demonstrating basic classroom signs.
- Host family sign-along events where children and parents learn together.
- Make sign language part of school-home communication (e.g., teachers can send notes home in English with ASL video explanations).

Working with Administration & Program Directors to Support ASL

One of the biggest barriers to implementing sign language in schools is a lack of administrative support. While individual teachers may be passionate about using ASL, they often face challenges when trying to get school-wide approval, funding, or professional development opportunities.

- Educate administrators on the benefits of signing (provide research, success stories, and statistics).
- Request ASL professional development training for teachers and staff (Signing Courses offers this!).
- Showcase student progress through videos or classroom demonstrations.
- Encourage schools to partner with Signing Courses to bring in ASL mentors.

- Propose adding ASL as a recognized communication tool in special education policies.

School-wide ASL programs are more effective when administrators and program directors actively support language access initiatives.

---

504 Plan Example: Ensuring Sign Language is Part of a Child's Educational Support Plan

For students with hearing loss, speech delays, or neurodiverse communication needs, sign language can be included as part of their formal education plan through a 504 Plan or an Individualized Education Program (IEP).

Example of a 504 Plan with ASL Integration

Student Profile:

Name: Alex
Grade: 2nd Grade
Diagnosis: Hearing loss, speech delay
Communication Needs: Requires ASL support for full classroom participation

Accommodations:

1. Use of ASL for instruction and communication support.
2. Teachers will incorporate Signing Courses Flashcards and Posters to reinforce daily signs.
3. Peers will be encouraged to learn basic ASL for classroom inclusion.
4. Access to ASL interpreter for assemblies, group discussions, and school events.
5. Regular check-ins with a speech-language pathologist or ASL specialist to assess language development.

Example 504 Plan for a 3-Year-Old with Speech Delay

Student Profile:

Name: Ethan

Age: 3 years old

Diagnosis: Speech delay

Communication Needs: Needs alternative communication strategies while developing verbal speech

Accommodations & Supports

1. **Use of ASL to Support Communication Development**

   - Ethan will be introduced to key ASL signs to express basic needs (e.g., "more," "help," "eat," "all done").
   - Signing Courses Flashcards and Posterswill be used daily in the classroom to reinforce sign language learning.
   - Educators and caregivers will model signs alongside verbal speech to encourage dual-language development.

2. **Visual Supports for Language Development**

   - ASL signs will be paired with pictures, gestures, and verbal prompts to create a multi-modal learning experience.
   - Classroom visual scheduleswill include signed instructions to aid comprehension.

3. **Classroom Integration of ASL for Peer Interaction**

   - Teachers will introduces imple signing activities so Ethan's peers can also learn basic signs.
   - Signing will be incorporated into circle time, transitions, and group play to ensure that Ethan feels included.

4. **Speech Therapy & Signing Integration**

- A speech-language pathologist (SLP) willc ollaborate with the teacher to reinforce both signing and verbal speech.
- ASL will be used as a bridge to verbal communication, reducing frustration while verbal skills develop.

5. **Family Engagement & Home Reinforcement**

- Parents will receive weekly ASL resources and video tutorialsfrom Signing Courses to practice at home.
- Families will be encouraged to use key signs during mealtime, play, and bedtime to support consistency.

By formalizing sign language support in 504 Plans and IEPs, educators ensure that ASL is not just a suggestion, but a guaranteed part of the child's educational success.

ASL in education is not a trend or a temporary tool—it is a necessary and effective way to support all students in communication, learning, and inclusion.

For sign language to truly make an impact, it must be:

- Embraced by families and educators together
- Embedded into daily classroom routines
- Supported by school administrators and program directors
- Recognized as a formal communication tool in educational support plans

By implementing these strategies, we set up students for success—giving them the communication skills, confidence, and inclusion they deserve.

Chapter 11: Simple Signs Lesson Plans – Engaging Activities for Early Learning

This chapter offers 18 easy-to-follow lesson plans designed for toddlers (ages 0-3) and preschoolers (ages 3-5), including two literacy-focused lessons using The Signing Courses materials. All lessons can be modified any way you want. Additionally, educators can create their own lesson plans using the Simple Signing Lesson Plan and Activity Templates included at the end of this book.

The lesson plans provide structured ASL activities that align with early childhood education frameworks, supporting:

- **Language & Communication Development** – Expanding vocabulary through sign language.
- **Cognitive Development** – Encouraging problem-solving, sequencing, and matching skills.
- **Social-Emotional Learning** – Helping children express relationships, emotions, and needs.
- **Fine & Gross Motor Skills** – Strengthening hand movements through signing activities.
- **Inclusion & Accessibility** – Making communication accessible for all children, regardless of ability.

"Sign language is not just a tool; it is a bridge to understanding and inclusion." Nyle DiMarco (Deaf Model, Activist, and Winner of 'America's Next Top Model')

Simple Signing Lesson Plans

My Main Signing Goal is...

_____

_____

_____

_____

Lesson 1: Sensory Sign Discovery

Purpose: Encourage communication through ASL while engaging the senses.

Materials Needed:

- A sensory bin filled with textured items (e.g., soft fabric, sand, plastic animals, wooden blocks).
- Signing Courses Flashcards or printed images of ASL signs related to the objects (e.g., "soft," "smooth," "animal").

Steps:

1. Introduce the sensory bin and encourage children to explore using their hands. 2. As they pick up different objects, teach them the corresponding ASL sign (e.g., sign "soft" while touching a fuzzy fabric).
3. Model the sign several times and encourage children to mimic it.
4. Use verbal reinforcement along with signs to create connections between the sensory experience and communication.

Adaptations:

- Use larger objects for children with fine motor challenges.
- Pair signs with verbal prompts and picture symbols for multi-modal learning.
- If a child is sensory-sensitive, allow them to explore one object at a time instead of a full sensory bin.

Lesson 2: Movement & Signs Adventure

Purpose: Build gross motor skills while introducing ASL action words.

Materials Needed:

- Visuals of ASL action words (e.g., "jump," "run," "spin").
- Open space for movement.

Steps:

1. Teach a few simple ASL signs for actions, demonstrating each movement (e.g., sign and jump).
2. Create a game where children perform the action while signing the word.
3. Play music or incorporate storytelling (e.g., "Let's spin like a top!" while signing "spin").

Adaptations:

- Offer seated movement options for children with mobility challenges (e.g., arm movements instead of jumping).
- Incorporate tactile feedback (e.g., clapping, stomping) for children with sensory needs.

Lesson 3: Picture-to-Sign Matching

Purpose: Develop language and matching skills through ASL.

Materials Needed:

- Pictures of familiar objects (e.g., toys, animals, food).
- ASL flashcards or printed images of ASL signs.
- Velcro board or magnetic board for matching.

Steps:

1. Display pictures of objects and their corresponding ASL signs.
2. Encourage children to match the pictures to the correct ASL sign card.
3. Model the sign and say the word each time a match is made.
4. Create a short story or simple sequence using the matched signs.

Adaptations:

- Use fewer matches for children who benefit from simpler tasks.
- Add real-life objects (e.g., a toy apple) for children who learn best through hands-on touch.

Lesson 4: Storytime with Signs

Purpose: Enhance comprehension and engagement during reading time with ASL.

Materials Needed:

- A simple, illustrated book (e.g., about animals, emotions, or daily routines).
- A list of ASL signs relevant to the story.

Steps:

1. Before reading, introduce a few key ASL signs from the story.
2. Read the book aloud, pausing to demonstrate ASL signs for important words (e.g., "dog," "eat").
3. Encourage children to mimic the signs as you read.
4. Re-read the story, focusing on a few signs at a time.
5. End with a discussion where children use the signs to talk about the book.

Adaptations:

- Use touch-and-feel books for sensory engagement.
- Pair ASL signs with gestures or props for children with limited motor skills.

Lesson 5: Feelings and Faces

Purpose: Teach emotional regulation and expression using ASL.

Materials Needed:

- Mirrors for children to see their facial expressions.
- Cards or pictures showing different emotions (e.g., happy, sad, excited, angry).
- Visuals of ASL signs for emotions.

Steps:

1. Show an emotion card and teach the corresponding ASL sign.
2. Encourage children to mimic the facial expression and sign while looking in the mirror.
3. Role-play scenarios where children identify emotions and use ASL signs to express how they feel.
4. Create a feelings chart to reinforce emotion vocabulary and signs.

Adaptations:

- Use tactile emotion symbols (e.g., smiley-face stickers) for children with visual impairments.
- Pair signs with verbal labels or sound effects for additional reinforcement.

Lesson 6: "Sing & Sign Circle Time" (Toddlers, Ages 1-3)

Purpose: Reinforce basic ASL signs through music and repetition.

Materials Needed:

- Signing Courses Flashcards for basic signs ("more," "eat," "drink," "play").
- A familiar song like *Twinkle, Twinkle Little Star* or *Wheels on the Bus*.

Steps:

1. Choose a song and introduce two to three signs that relate to the lyrics.
2. Sing the song slowly, modeling the signs while singing.
3. Encourage children to copy the signs as they listen.
4. Repeat the song, letting children lead the signs as they learn.

Adaptations:

- Use hand-over-hand guidance for children with motor delays.
- Choose high-energy songs to keep active toddlers engaged.
- Incorporate simple instruments (e.g., maracas, bells) for additional sensory input.

Lesson 7: "Sign & Seek" (Toddlers, Ages 1-3)

Purpose: Strengthen ASL vocabulary through a movement-based scavenger hunt.

Materials Needed:

- Flashcards or printed pictures of ASL signs for common objects (e.g., table, book, sit/chair).
- Real-life objects to match the signs.

Steps:

1. Place objects around the room, ensuring they are easy for toddlers to find.
2. Hold up a flashcard and model the sign for that object (e.g., sign "table" while holding the table card).
3. Say, "Can you find the table?" and encourage children to retrieve the correct item.
4. Once they bring the item, reinforce the sign before moving to the next round.

Adaptations:

- Allow children to point instead of retrieving objects if mobility is limited.
- Use real objects instead of flashcards for children who need tactile learning.

Lesson 8: "Sign & Storytime" (Toddlers, Ages 0-3)

Purpose: Introduce early signing alongside literacy for preverbal toddlers.

Materials Needed:

- A simple board book with high-contrast images.
- Family Signs Poster and Flashcards and others that match key words from the book ("mom," "dad," "dog," "love").

Steps:

1. Sit toddlers in a semi-circle or on a rug and introduce the book.
2. Show the first picture, sign the key word, and say it aloud.
3. Encourage toddlers to imitate the sign while pointing to the picture.
4. Repeat for each page, reinforcing the same 3-4 key signs throughout the story.

Adaptations:

- Use touch-and-feel books for sensory engagement.
- Offer ASL song breaks between reading sessions to keep toddlers engaged.

Lesson 9: "Sign & Rhyme Literacy" (Preschoolers, Ages 3-5)

Purpose: Strengthen early reading skills through ASL-supported rhyming activities.

Materials Needed:

- Any Signing Courses Posters for rhyming pairs (e.g., "cat" and "hat,").
- A large pocket chart or board for word matching.

Steps:

1. Introduce two rhyming words and demonstrate their ASL signs.

2. Say the words together and emphasize their ending sounds.

3. Show the flashcards and ask children to match the rhyming words.

4. Reinforce the signs as children say the words aloud.

5. Create a short ASL rhyme or chant using the words.

Adaptations:

- Use tactile letter cards for children with visual impairments.

- Introduce fingerspelling for older preschoolers ready for letter recognition.

Lesson 10: "Sign Your Name" (Preschoolers, Ages 3-5, Literacy-Focused)

Purpose: Introduce fingerspelling and name recognition through ASL.

Materials Needed:

A Signing Courses ASL Alphabet Poster.
Name cards with each child's name written in large letters.

Steps:

1. Teach children how to sign the first letter of their name using fingerspelling.

2. Show them their name card and have them trace the letters with their finger.

3. Model how to sign each letter of their name slowly.

4. Encourage children to try fingerspelling their full name with assistance.

5. Practice each day, celebrating progress.

Adaptations:

- Use hand-over-hand support for fine motor assistance.
- Let children decorate their name cards to personalize their learning experience.
- Let children play pretend restaurant where they order snacks using ASL.

Lesson 11: "Playtime Signs" – Using Signs During Interactive Play

Objective: Teach children to communicate during playtime using simple ASL signs.

Materials Needed:

- School Signs Flashcards & Poster
- Toys (blocks, stuffed animals, balls)

Steps:

1. Introduce the signs for "play," "outside," "help," "wait," and "" using the flashcards.
2. During play, hold up a ball and model "ball" before rolling it to the child.
3. When a child needs assistance (e.g., building a block tower), model "help" before offering support.
4. Play a freeze dance game, using "wait" and "more" signs while playing music. 5. Encourage peer interaction by prompting children to ask for toys or help using signs.

Adaptations for Ages 3-5:

- Incorporate group games (e.g., Red Light, Green Light) using "wait" and "more" signs.
- Teach children to request turns using ASL (e.g., signing *"my turn"* before taking a toy).
- Introduce fingerspelling for short words like "play" to strengthen early literacy skills.

Lesson 12: "Feelings and Expressions" – Signing Emotions

Objective: Help children identify and express emotions using ASL signs.

Materials Needed:

- Emotions Signs Flashcards & Poster
- Mirrors for children to see their expressions
- Picture cards with different emotions (happy, sad, angry, excited)

Steps:

1. Show flashcards for "happy," "sad," "mad," and "love." Model each sign with an exaggerated facial expression.
2. Have children look in the mirror and copy the sign while making the matching expression.
3. Play an emotion-matching game by holding up an emotion card and having children sign what they see.
4. Read a short story about emotions and pause to sign key feelings as they appear in the book.
5. Sing a Feelings Song (*If You're Happy and You Know It*), using ASL signs for emotions.

Adaptations for Ages 3-5:

- Add role-play activities where children act out scenarios and sign how they feel.
- Teach expanded phrases like *"I feel happy"* or *"She is sad."*
- Introduce a classroom "Emotion Board" where children sign and point to how they feel each morning.

Lesson 13: "Bedtime Routine" – Using ASL for Transitions

Objective: Help children recognize and use ASL signs for common bedtime routines.

Materials Needed:

- Common First Signs Flashcards & Poster
- Stuffed animals or dolls for role-playing bedtime routines
- Soft music to create a calming environment

Steps:

1. Introduce the signs "sleep," "bath," "sleep/bed," and "I love you" using flashcards and posters.
2. Use a doll or stuffed animal to model a bedtime routine, signing each step.
3. Encourage children to act out bedtime steps with their own dolls while signing.
4. Sing a lullaby while signing "sleep" and "goodnight" to reinforce the routine.
5. Provide a quiet, cozy reading space where children can look at picture books about bedtime while practicing signs.

Adaptations for Ages 3-5:

- Have children create a bedtime sequence using ASL signs.
- Teach full bedtime phrases (e.g., *"Time for bed," "Brush your teeth,"* or *"Go to sleep"*)
- Let children use a sign-based bedtime chart to track their nightly routine.

Lesson 14: "My Needs" – Helping Children Express Basic Requests

Objective: Teach children to express common requests and needs using ASL.

Materials Needed:

- Common First Signs Flashcards & Poster
- Real-life objects to represent needs (e.g., food, cup, blanket)

Steps:

1. Introduce the signs "help," "want," "more," "stop," and "thank you."
2. Model scenarios where children may need help and encourage them to sign for assistance.
3. Play a "What Do You Need?" game, where children pick an item and sign the request.
4. Reinforce signs in everyday situations (e.g., during snack time, encourage them to sign "more" instead of pointing).
5. Praise and reinforce when children use signs instead of whining or crying.

Adaptations for Ages 3-5:

- Introduce sentence-building (e.g., *"I want more" or "Can you help me?"*).
- Play a role-playing activity where children take turns asking for different objects.
- Encourage children to sign their needs throughout the day in classroom settings.

Lesson 15: Healthy Habits – Learning Health & Doctor Signs

Objective: Teach children to use ASL signs for health and doctor visits to support daily routines.

Materials Needed:

- Health Signs Poster & Flashcards
- Small items representing a trip to the doctor (headache, medicine, fever)
- Stuffed animals or dolls for role-playing

Steps:

1. Introduce the Signs – Show flashcards and model "wash," "brush teeth," "clean," "sick," "help."
2. Role-Play a Morning Routine – Use a doll or stuffed animal to act out a trip to see the doctor.
3. Mirror Practice – Encourage children to look in a mirror and sign "better" while leaving the doctor office.
4. Clean Up Game – Scatter small objects found at a doctor's office, and have children sign "clean" as they put items away.
5. Sing a Hygiene Song (*This is the way we wash our hands*) while signing.

Adaptations for Ages 3-5:

- Have children act out their own hygiene routine and sign each step.
- Teach expanded phrases like "I need help" or "I feel sick."
- Create a classroom hygiene chart where children sign when they complete tasks (e.g., washing hands).

Lesson 16: What's the Weather? Learning Weather Signs

Objective: Teach children ASL weather signs and help them recognize weather changes in their environment.

Materials Needed:

- Weather Signs Poster & Flashcards
- Pictures or real examples of different weather conditions (sun, clouds, rain, snow)
- Sensory materials (spray bottle for rain, fan for wind, warm lamp for sun)

Steps:

1. Introduce Weather Signs – Use flashcards to teach "sun," "rain," "wind," "snow," "cloud."
2. Look Outside & Sign – Ask, *"What's the weather today?"* and encourage children to sign the correct word.
3. Sensory Exploration – Let children feel the "rain" (light spray bottle mist) or "wind" (fan blowing on their hand) while signing.
4. Weather Matching Game – Show a weather flashcard, and have children match it to a real object (e.g., cotton balls for clouds).
5. Sing a Weather Song (*It's Raining, It's Pouring*) while signing along.

Adaptations for Ages 3-5:

- Have children draw today's weather and label it with ASL signs.
- Teach fingerspelling for short weather words (sun, rain, clouds).
- Play a weather forecaster role-play game, where children pretend to give the day's weather report in ASL.

Lesson 17: Animal Fun – Learning Animal Signs Through Movement

Objective: Teach children ASL signs for common animals using movement and sound play.

Materials Needed:

- Animal Signs Poster & Flashcards
- Stuffed animals or animal figurines
- Open space for movement activities

Steps:

1. Introduce the Signs – Show flashcards for "dog," "cat," "cow," "bird," "horse," "pig."
2. Animal Sounds & Signs – Make an animal sound and have children guess the sign (e.g., *"Moo!"* sign "cow").
3. Move Like an Animal – Encourage children to hop like a bunny, crawl like a cat, or flap like a bird while signing.
4. Find the Animal Game – Hide animal toys around the room, and have children sign the name when they find one.
5. Sing a Song (*Old MacDonald Had a Farm*), signing the animal names instead of singing them.

Adaptations for Ages 3-5:

- Have children describe animal characteristics using ASL (e.g., *"The dog is big."*).
- Teach fingerspelling for animal names.
- Play "What am I?" – One child acts like an animal while others guess the sign.

Making Signing a Natural Part of Learning

These lesson plans are designed to scaffold learning and help educators naturally integrate ASL into their curriculum. Using the Simple Signing Lesson Plan Templates, teachers can adapt activities to fit their classroom needs and developmental levels.

- Builds foundational communication skills for preverbal and emerging verbal children.

- Encourages social-emotional growth by allowing children to express emotions and needs.
- Aligns with early learning standards in literacy, cognitive development, and classroom interaction.

By consistently using sign language, children gain an accessible, engaging, and meaningful way to communicate, setting them up for language success and inclusion.

Keep signing, keep learning, and keep making language accessible for all children!

And most importantly—*keep sharing the magic of simple signing.*

SIMPLE SIGNS

ACTIVITY

WORKBOOK

POSTERS AND FLASHCARDS

To purchase the Signing Courses Simple Signs posters and flashcards that complement this product, simply scan the QR code for an instant purchase and PDF download. **For educators and schools interested in placing large physical orders of sanitizing-safe and tear-resistant materials, please reach out to us.**

Want the ASL Materials for FREE?

We appreciate your support! As a thank you, we're gifting you our entire collection of Posters & Flashcards, as well as The Signing Courses Circle membership—FREE! Here's how to claim your gift:

1. Write a review on Amazon or Google about The Magic of Simple Signing.
2. Copy your review once it's posted.
3. Email us at support@signingcourses.com with your review attached.
4. Receive your exclusive coupon code for FREE checkout!

That's it! Your honest feedback helps us spread the magic of signing, and in return, you'll have instant access to powerful learning tools for FREE!
Email us today and start signing with confidence!

SCAN HERE OR VISIT WWW.SIGNINGCOURSES.COM

COMMON FIRST SIGNS

Sign, and color!

Wait

Sign, and color!

Sign, and color!

Sign, and color!

Help

Sign, and color!

All Done/Finished

Sign, and color!

Sign, and color!

Eat/ Food

Sign, and color!

Milk

Sign, and color!

Please

Sign, and color!

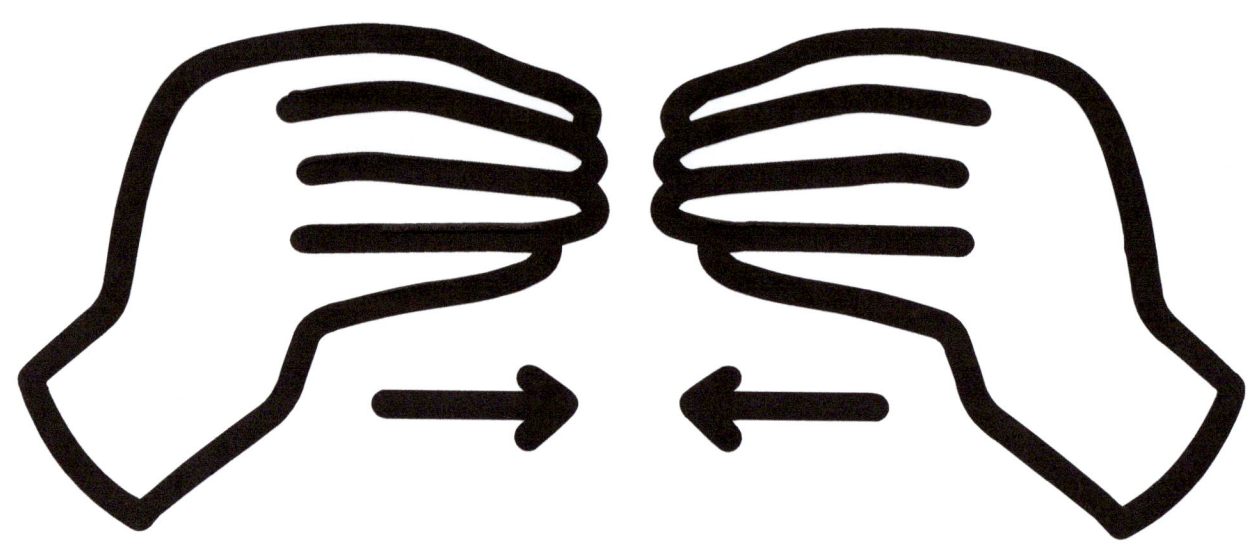

Sign, and color!

Toilet/Bathroom

Sign, and color!

Drink

Matching Signs

Can you draw a line to the matching sign?

Drink

More

More

Please

Toilet/Bathroom

Drink

Please

Toilet/Bathroom

Matching Words and Signs

Milk
Juice
Water

More
Eat/Food
Milk

Matching Words and Signs

More

Thank You

Water

Please

Sleep

All Done/Finished

Matching Words and Signs

More
Drink
Help

I Love You
Please
Sleep

Matching Words and Signs

More

Wait

Help

All
Done/Finished

Drink

Sleep/Bed

SCHOOL

School

SIGNS

Sign, and color!

Sit

Sign, and color!

Share

Sign, and color!

SCHOOL BUS

School

Sign, and color!

Table

Sign, and color!

Teach

Sign, and color!

Work

Sign, and color!

Friend

Sign, and color!

Learn

Sign, and color!

Book

Sign, and color!

Play

Sign, and color!

Outside

Sign, and color!

Write

SIGNING courses

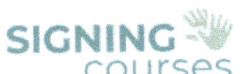

I Know The Picture

Look at the sign. Circle the picture that matches the sign. Then, you can color the picture.

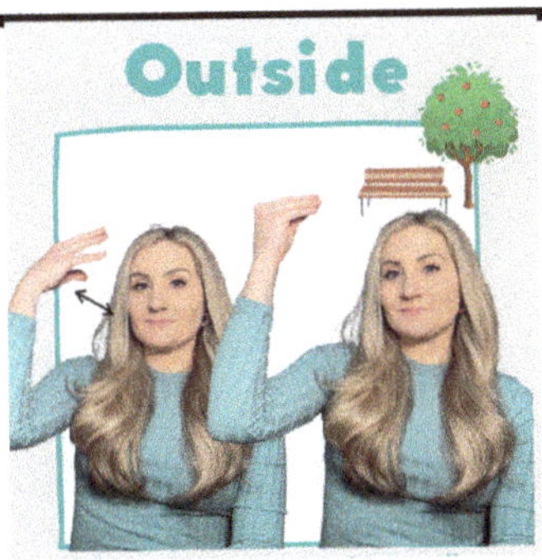
Outside

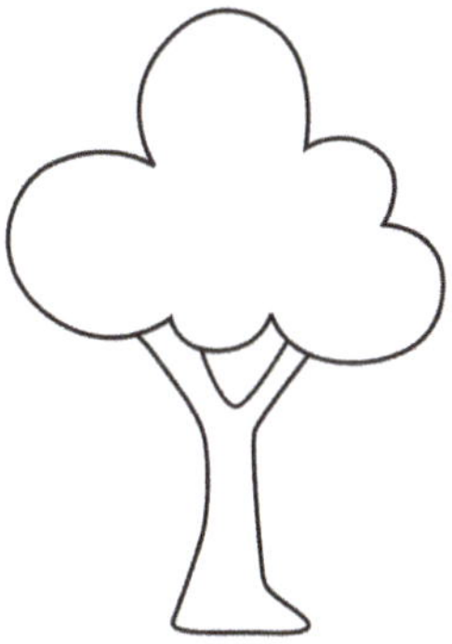

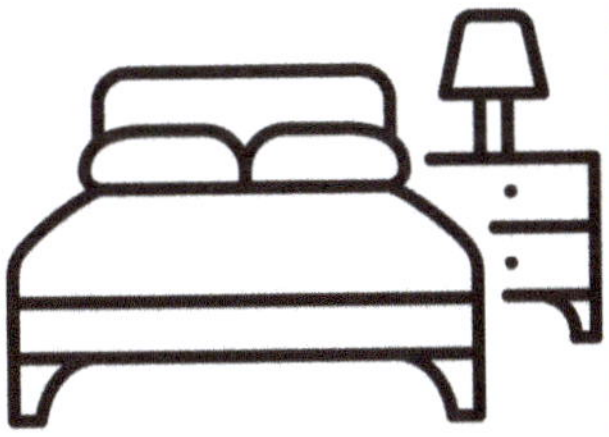

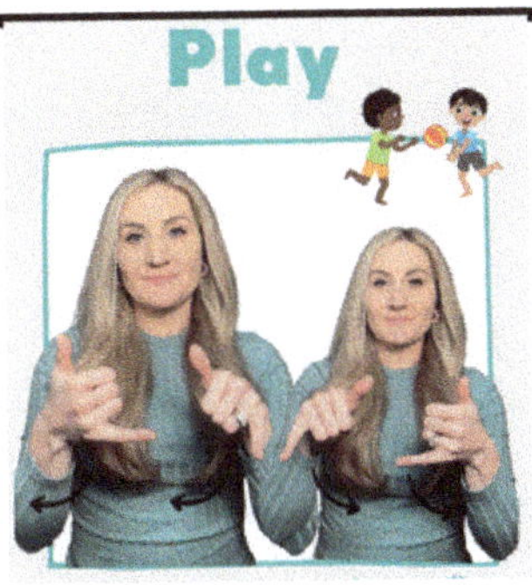
Play

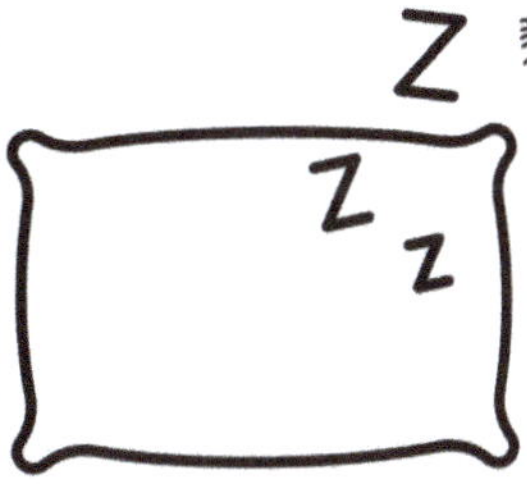
Z
Z
Z

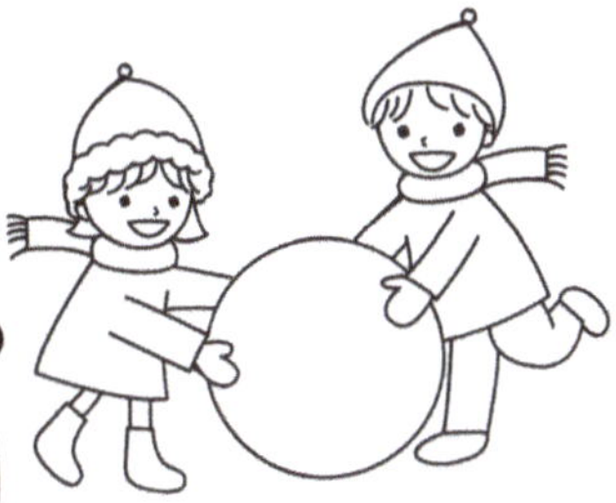

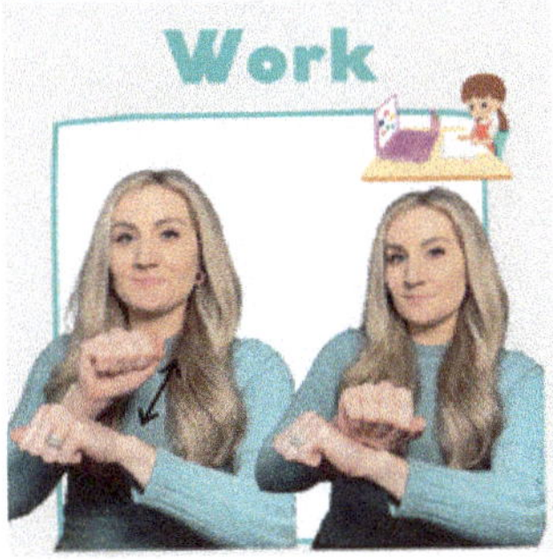
Work

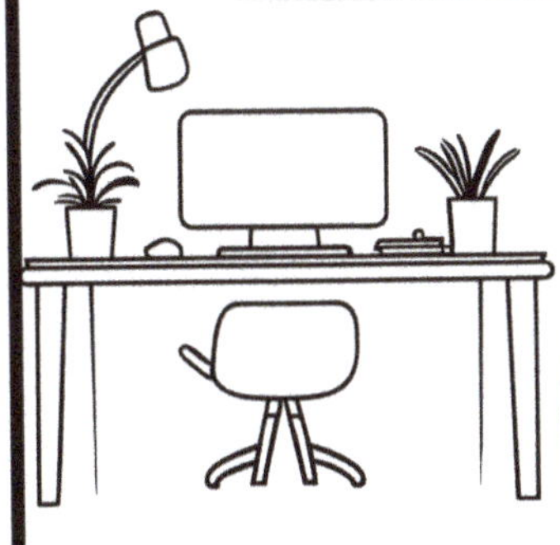

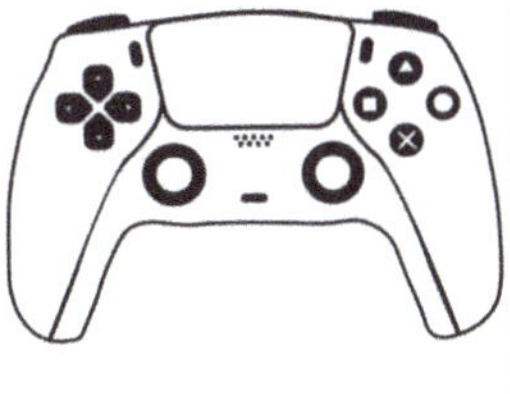

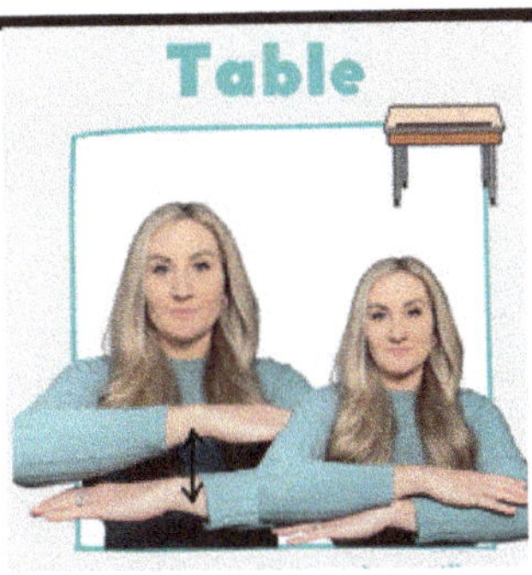
Table

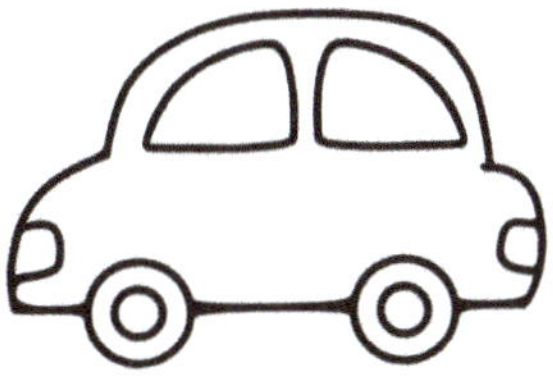

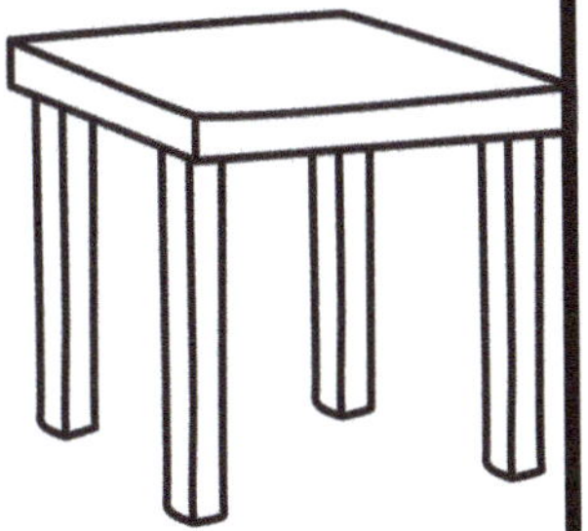

I Know The Picture

Look at the sign. Circle the picture that matches the sign. Then, you can color the picture.

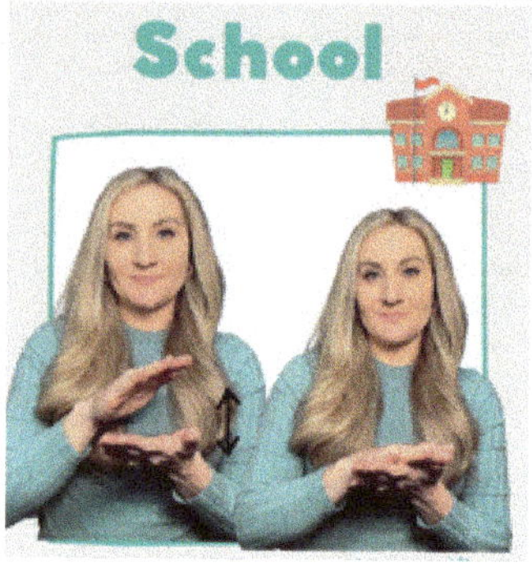

School

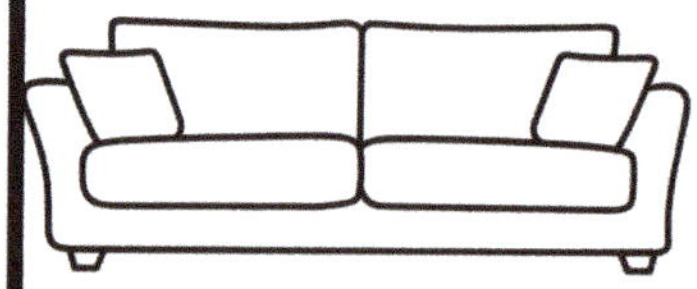

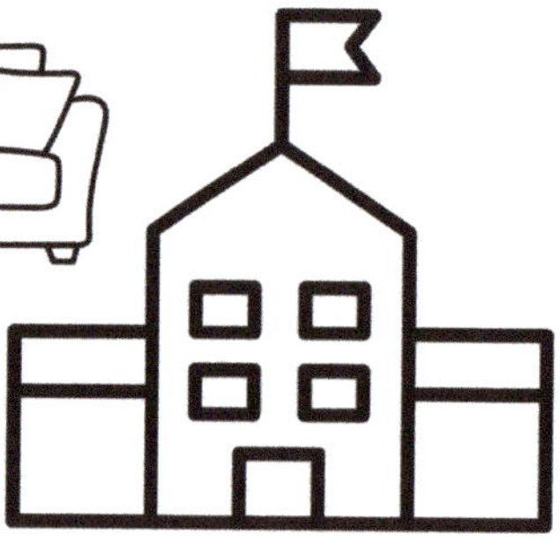

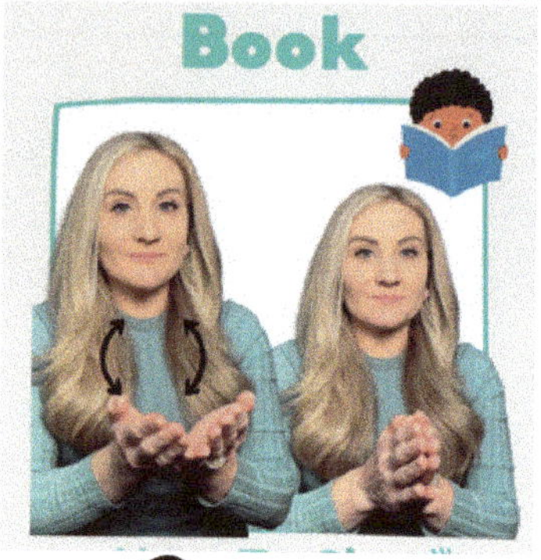

Book

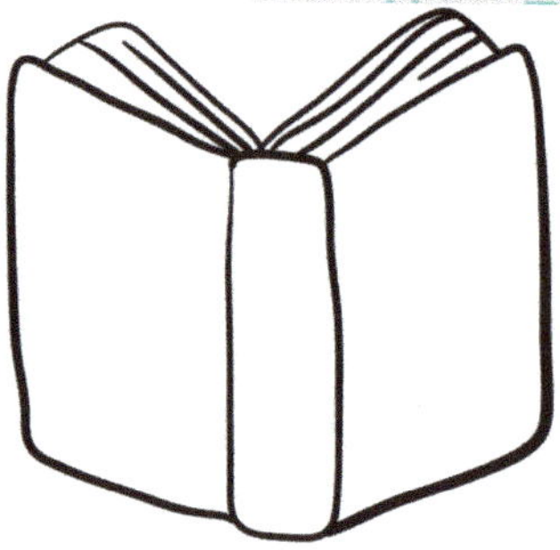

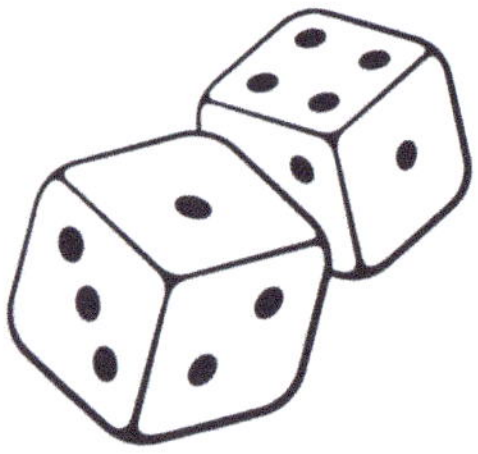

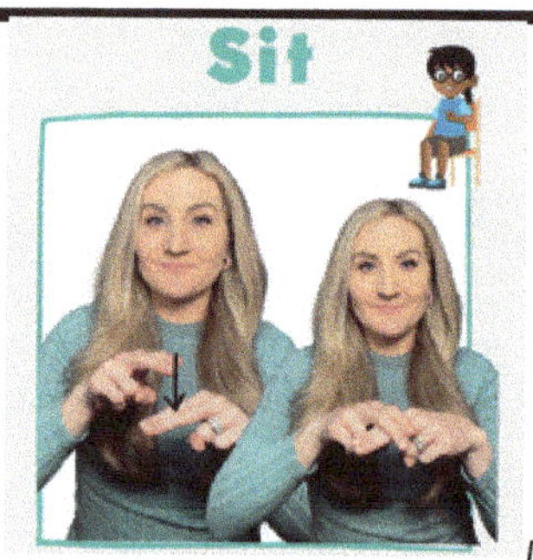

Sit

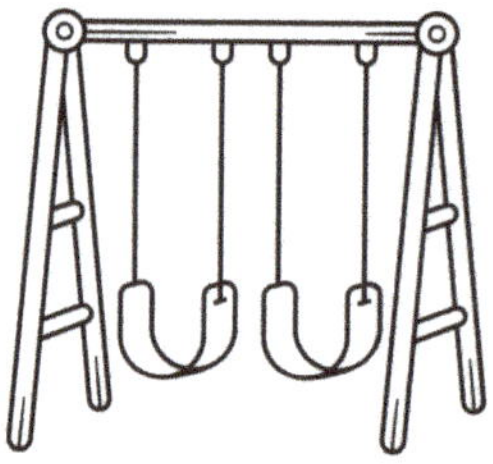

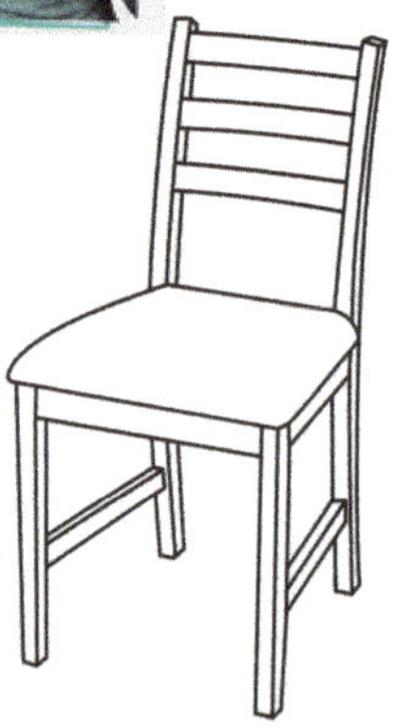

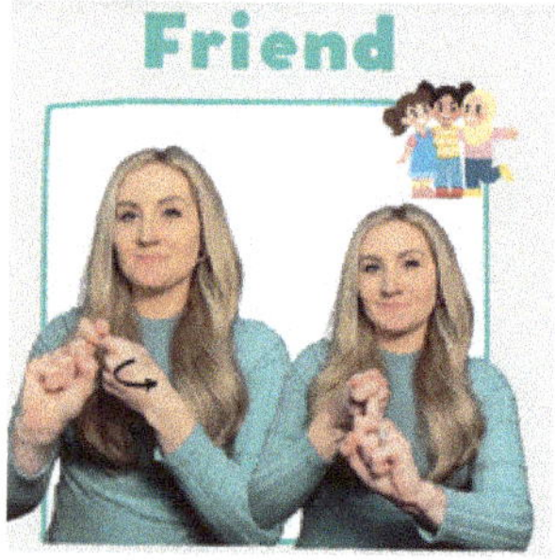

Friend

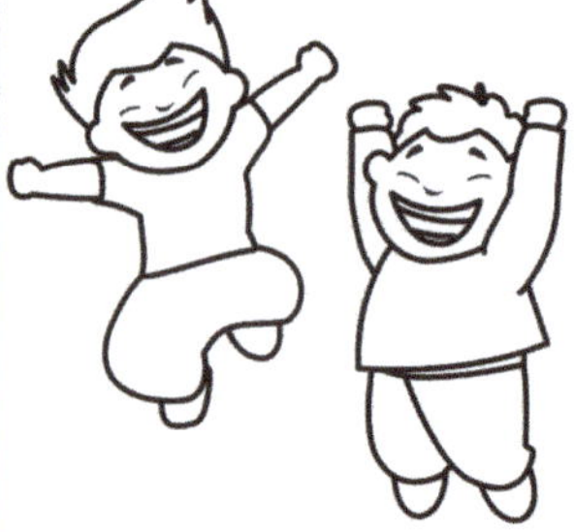

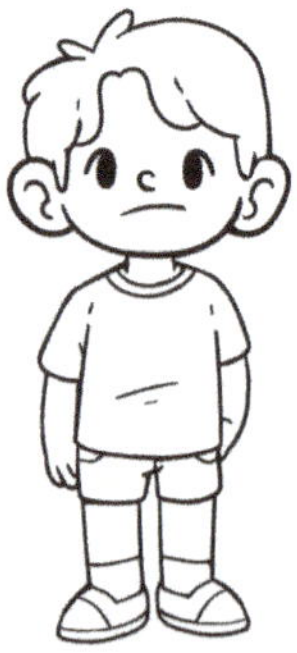

Finish The Picture

Use your imagination to finish the rest of this drawing of a book.

Use your imagination to finish the rest of this drawing of a school.

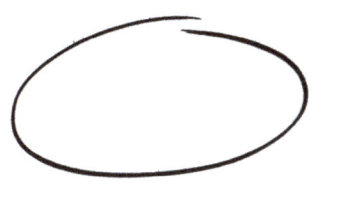

NUMBER

5, Five

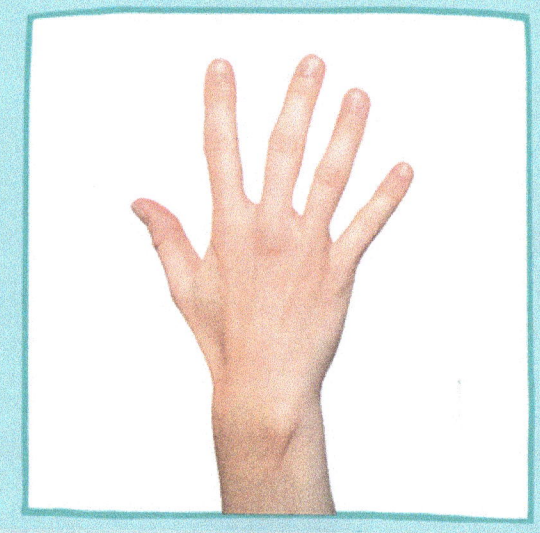

SIGNS

Matching Numbers and Signs

Can you match the signing hand to the number?

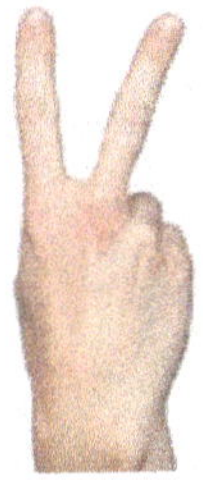

1

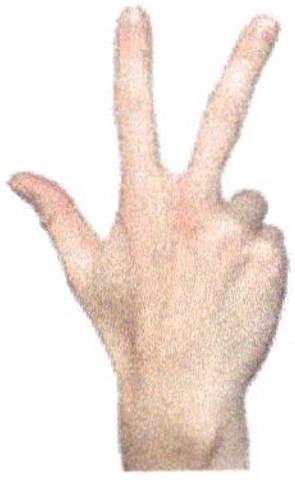

2

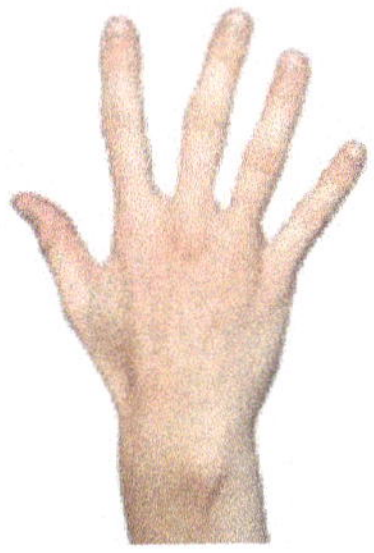

3

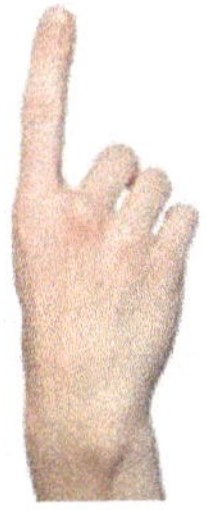

4

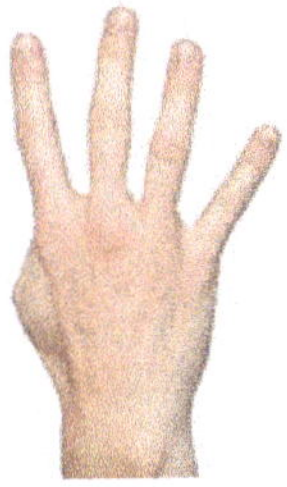

5

Matching Signs

Can you find the matching number hands?

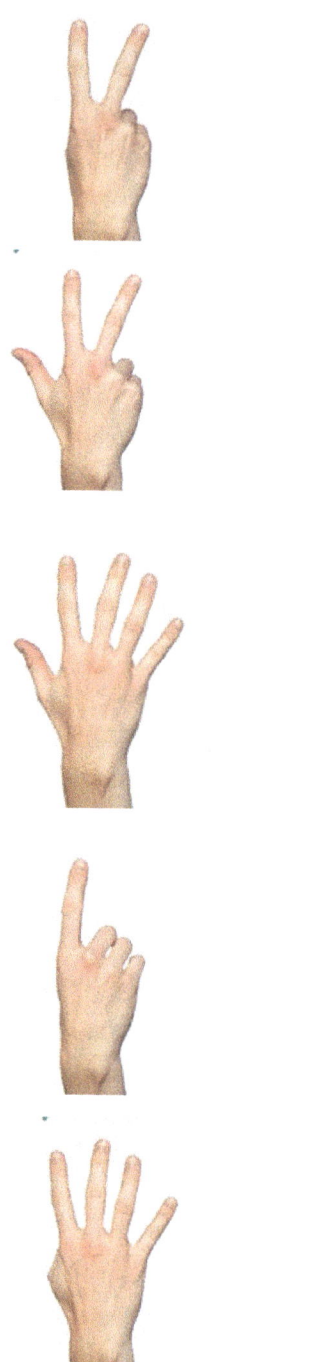
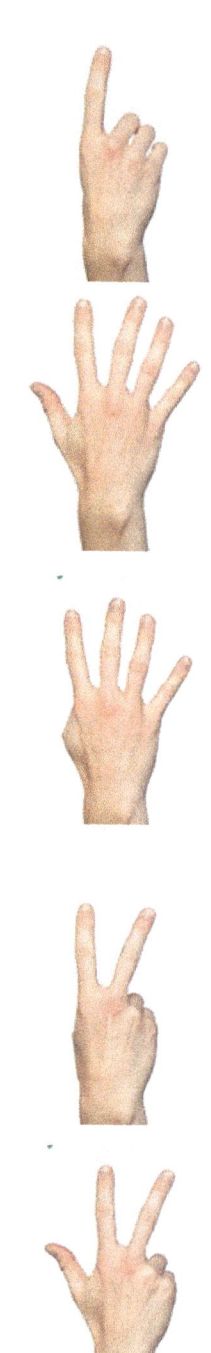

Count and Color

Count and color the exact number of unicorns that match the sign

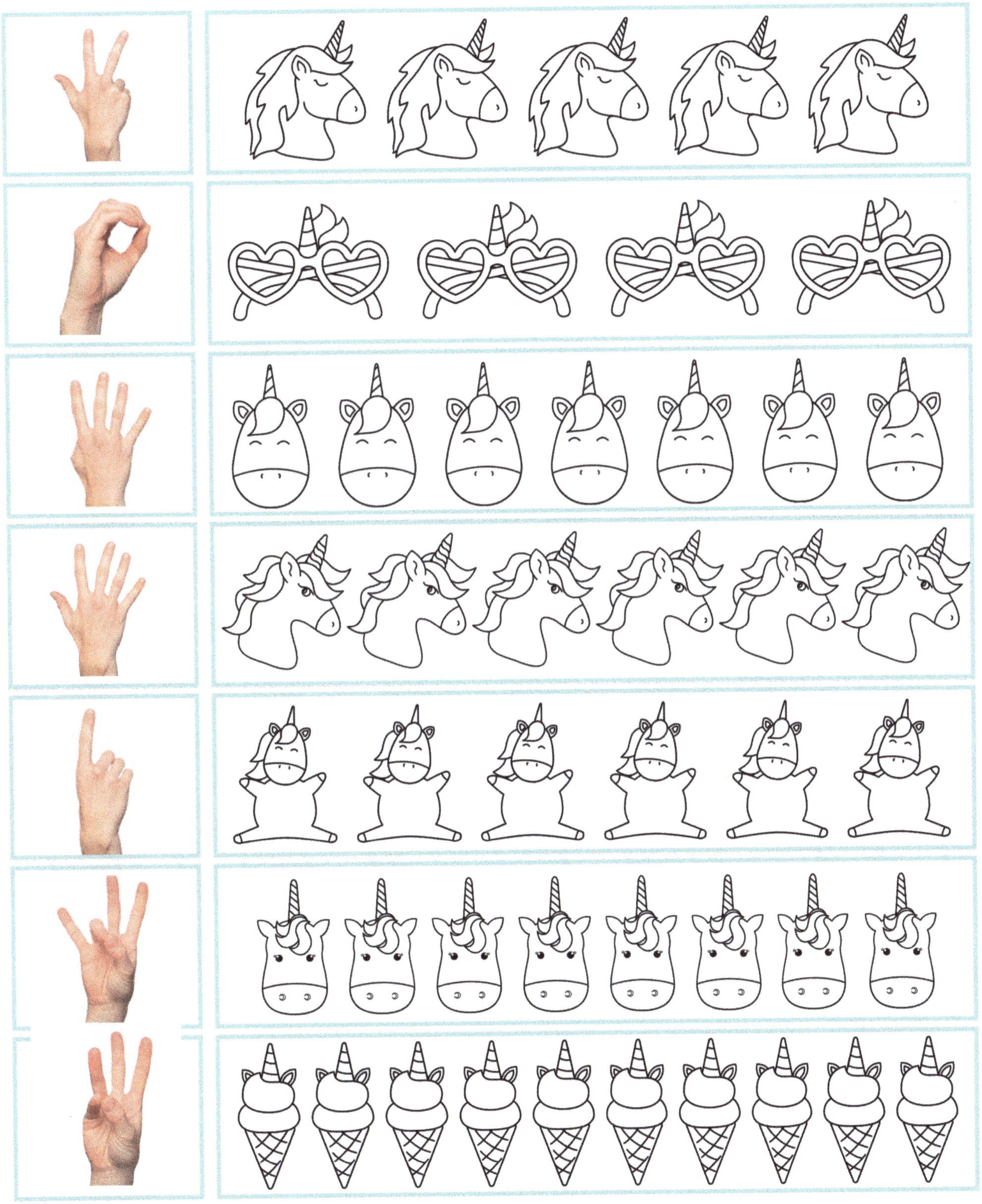

SIGNING courses

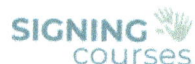

Count and Color

Count and color the exact number of unicorns that match the sign.

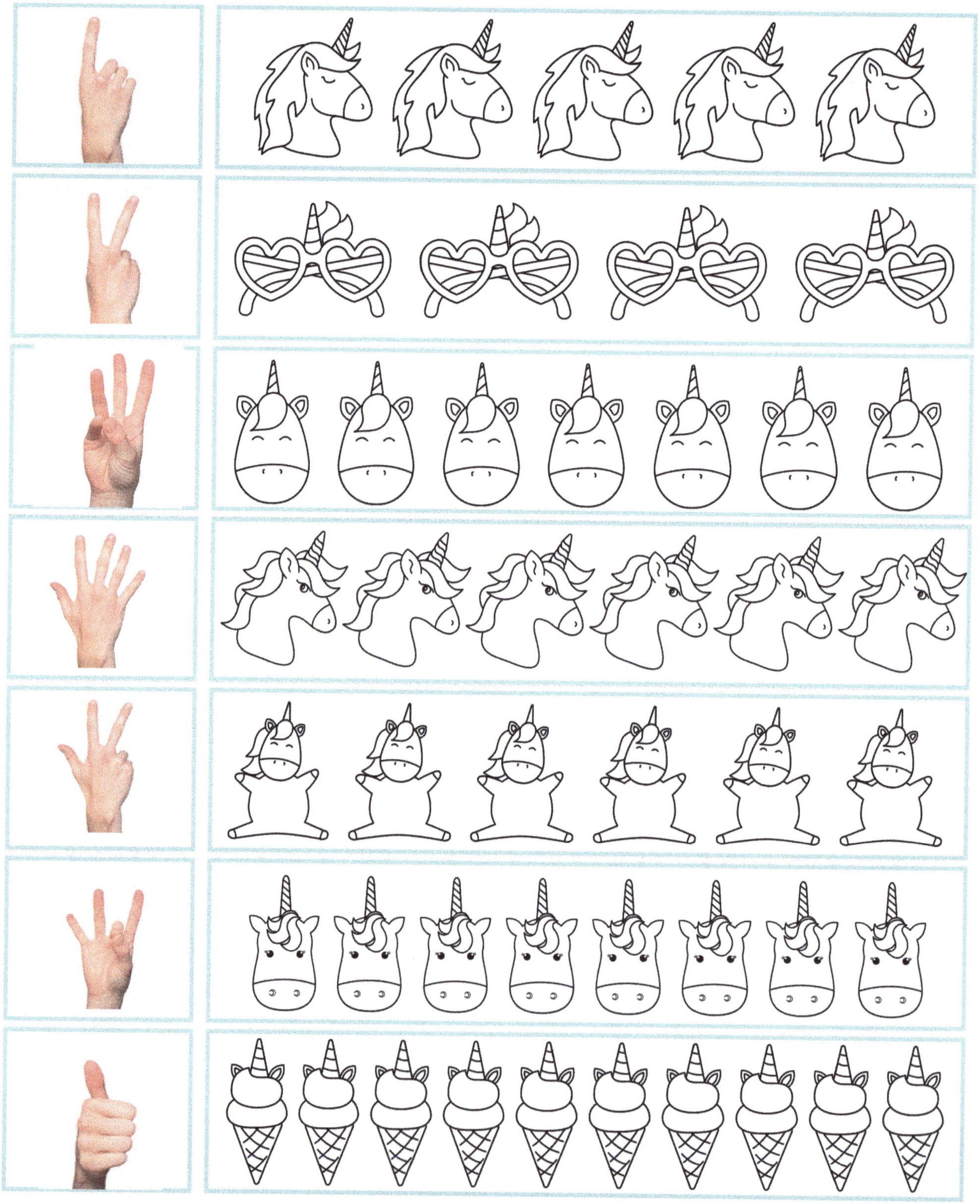

SIGNING courses

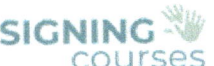

Count and Match

Match the number sign to the dinosaurs.

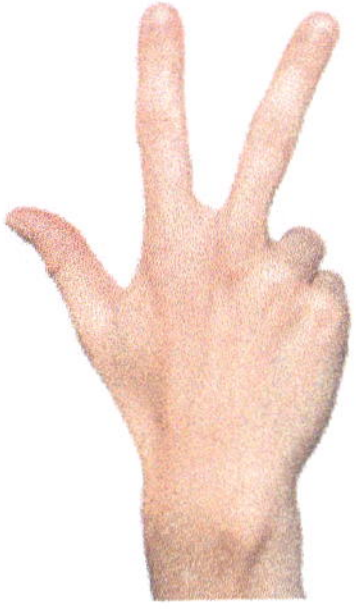

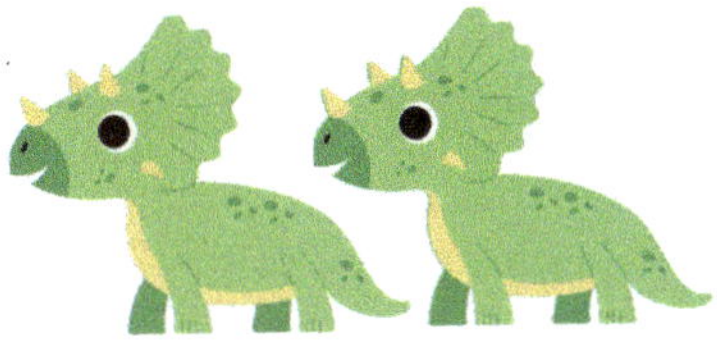

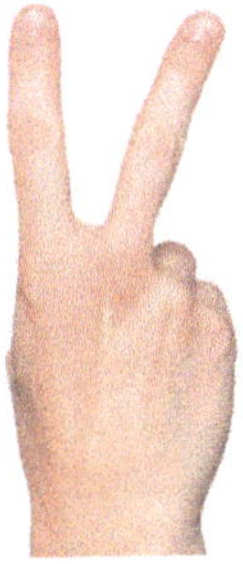

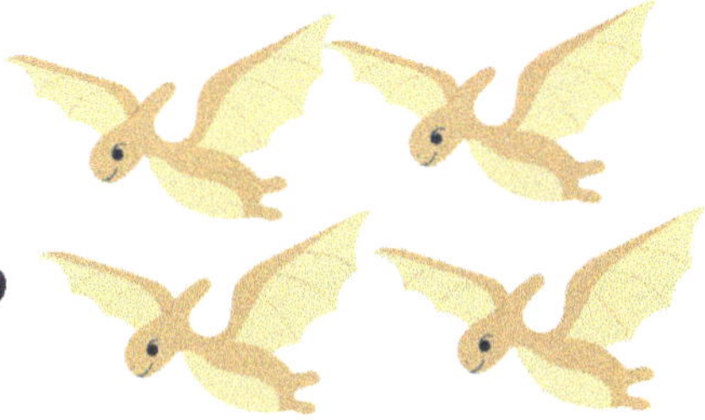

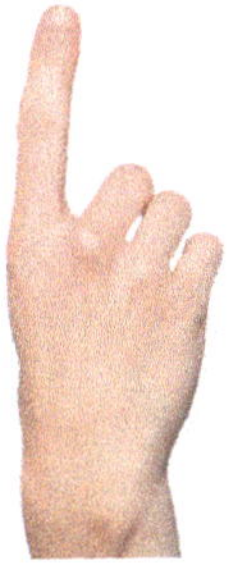

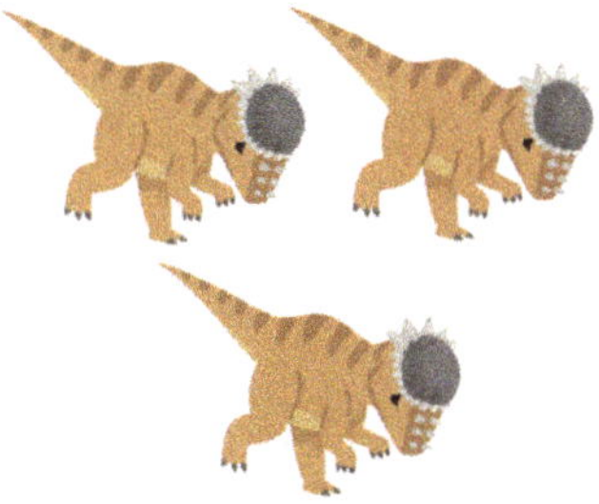

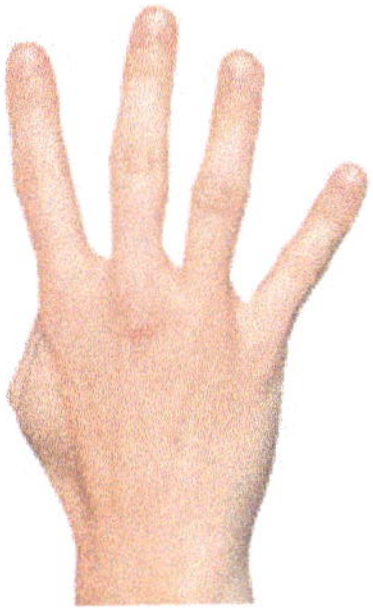

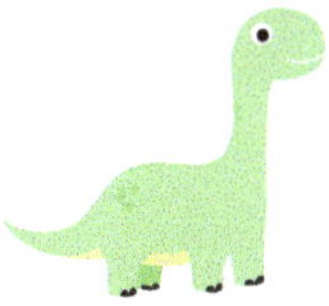

Count and Match

Count the dinosaurs and match the number sign.

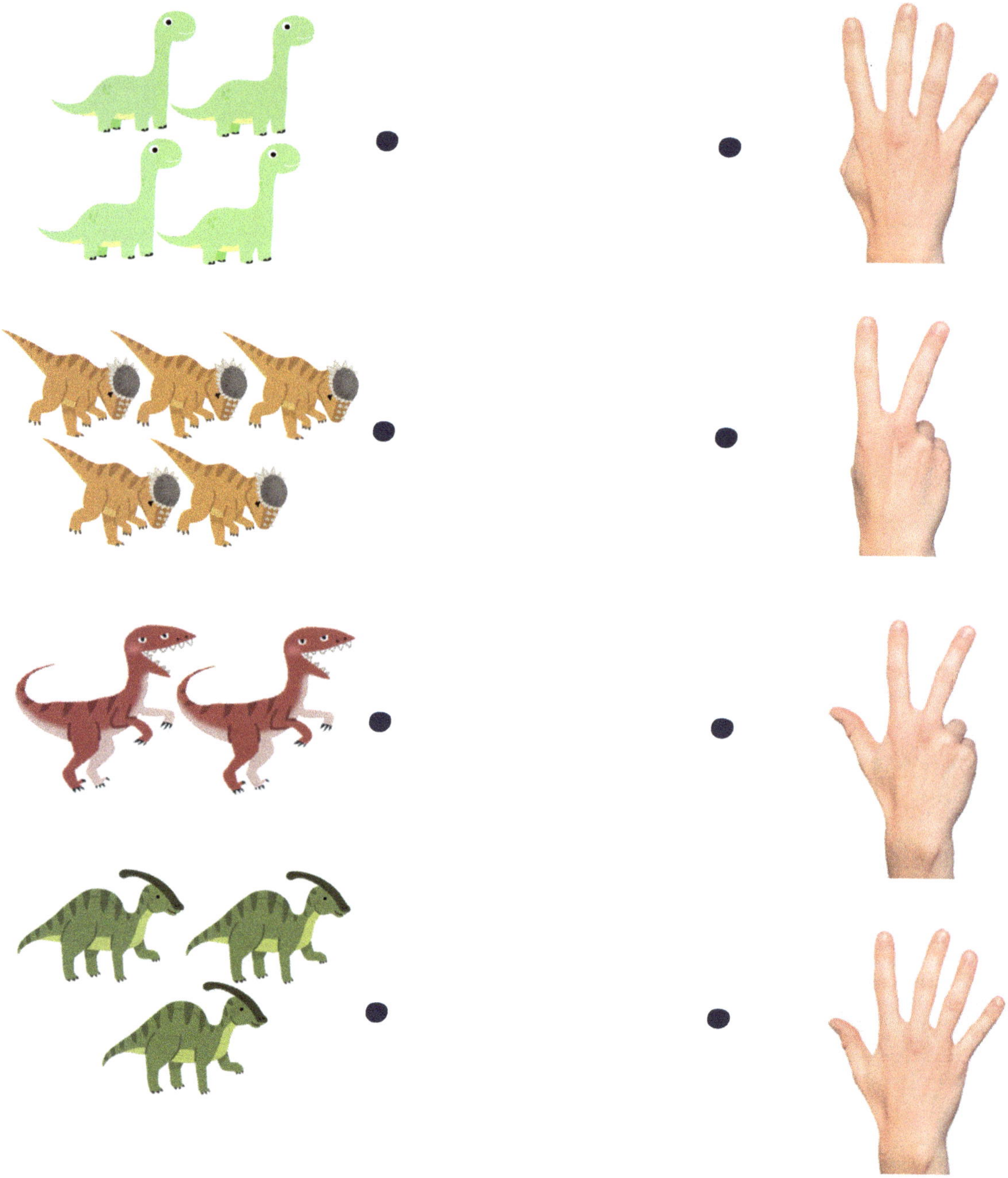

Let's Count!

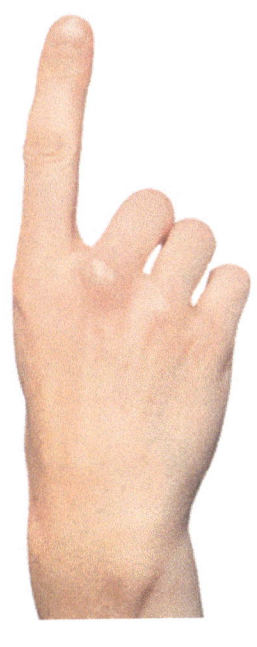

Let's Count!

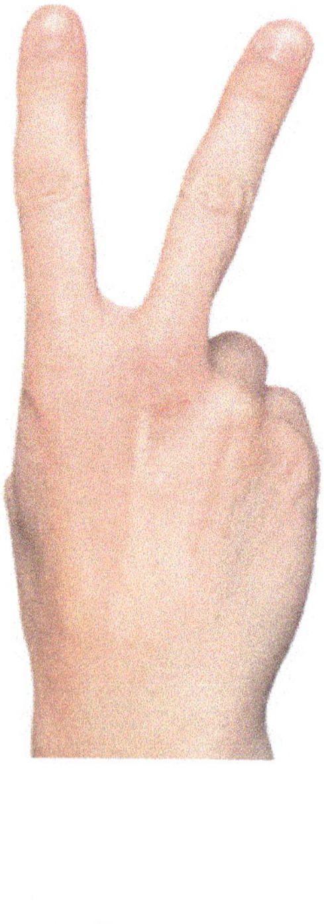

Let's Count!

3

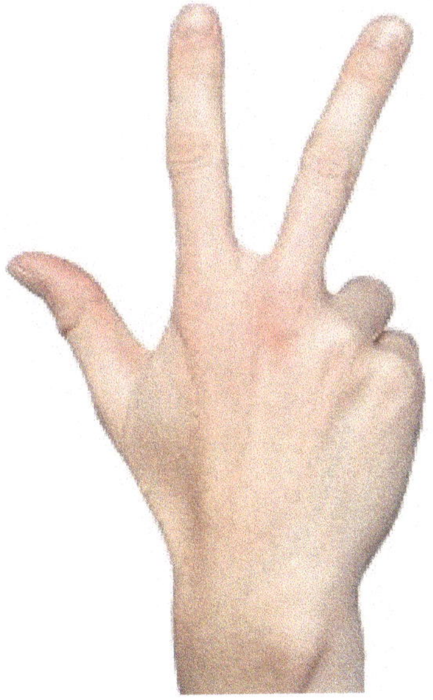

Let's Count!

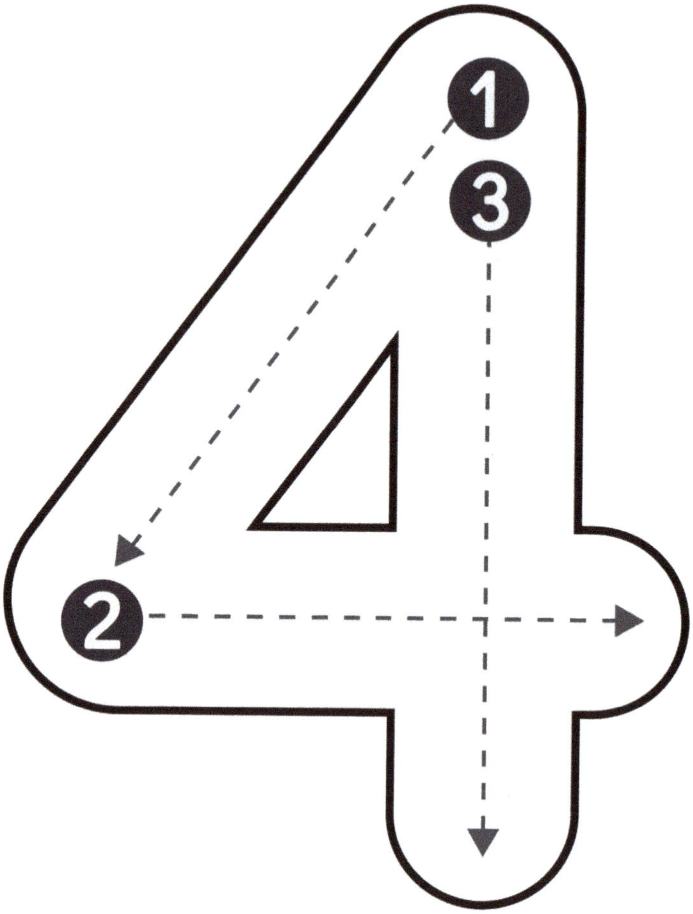

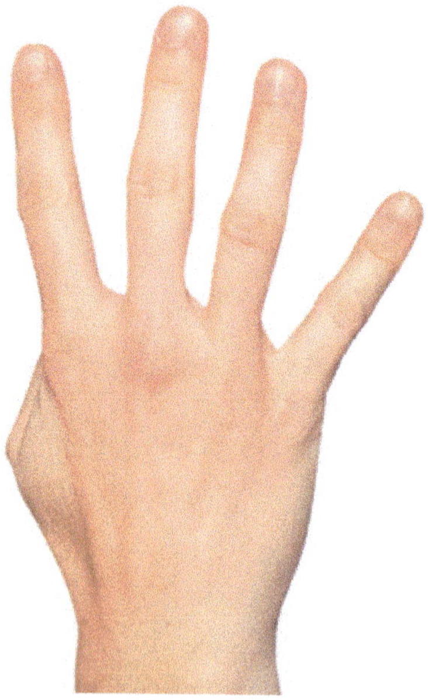

Let's Count!

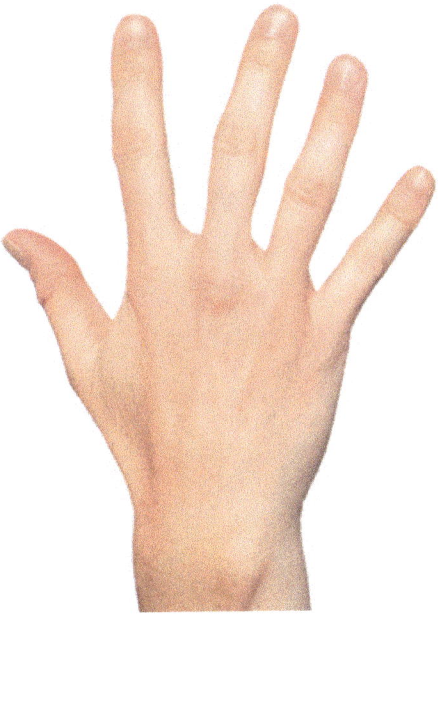

Let's Count!

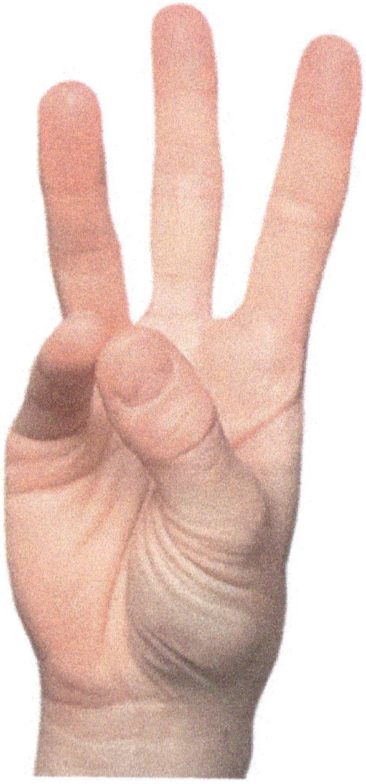

Let's Count!

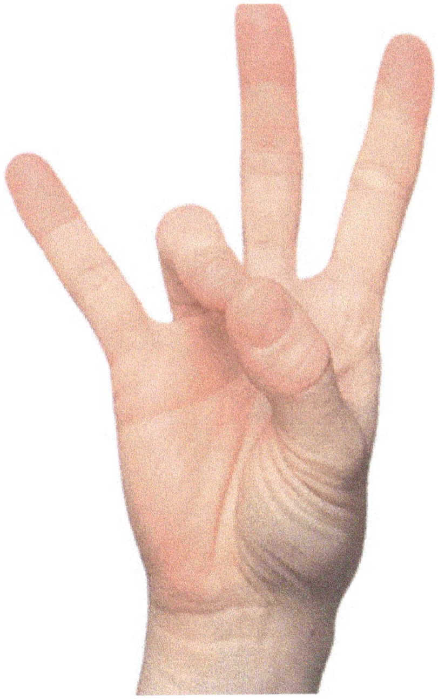

Let's Count!

8

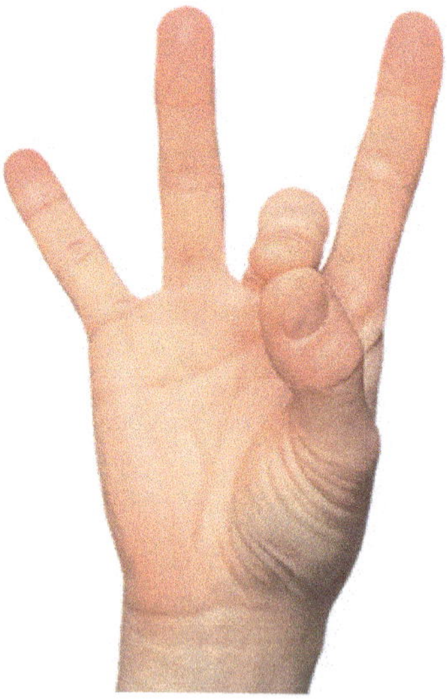

Let's Count!

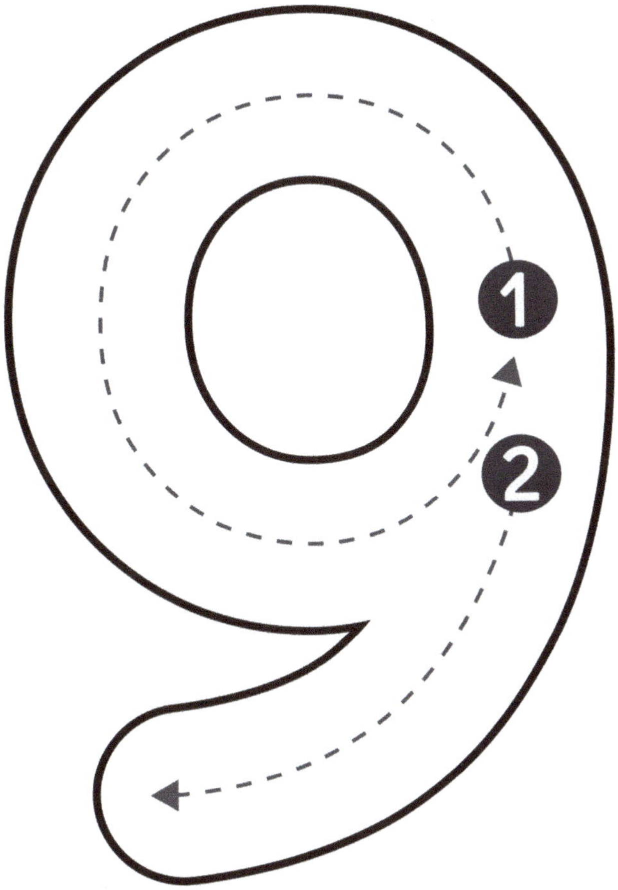

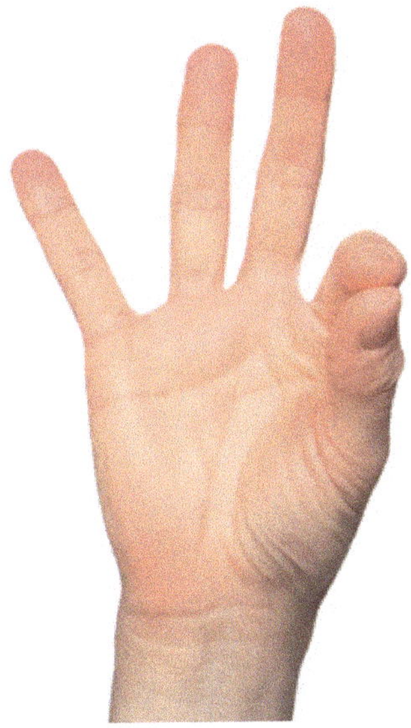

Let's Count!

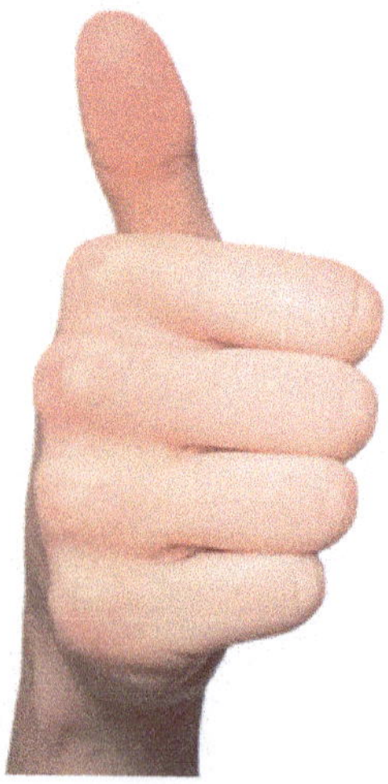

10

COLOR

Color

SIGNS

Matching Colors

green

yellow

orange

blue

red

pink

Matching Colors

red

yellow

orange

blue

red

pink

Matching Colors

blue

green

orange

brown

red

pink

Matching Colors

Purple

pink
purple
orange

White

white
red
yellow

Matching Colors

Black

yellow
red
Black

Brown

blue
brown
green

Red

Cherries

Apple

Strawberry

Ladybug

Orange

Orange

Carrot

Squash

Tiger

Yellow

Banana

Corn

Sun

Bee

Green

Broccoli

Caterpillar

Frog

Tree

Blue

Butterfly

Whale

Bird

Crayon

Purple

Grapes

Eggplant

Lavender

Octopus

Brown

Wood

Pretzel

Bear

Deer

Black

Bat

Spider

Shoes

Cat

Pink

Rose

Donut

Flamingo

Pig

ANIMAL

Animal

SIGNS

Sign, and color!

Lion

Sign, and color!

Monkey

Sign, and color!

Dog

Sign, and color!

Horse

Sign, and color!

Sheep

Sign, and color!

Cow

Sign, and color!

Bird

Sign, and color!

Duck

Sign, and color!

Tiger

Sign, and color!

Cat

Sign, and color!

Pig

ANIMAL

What is your favorite animal?

Draw it!

Animal Signs Puzzles

Print, cut and start puzzling

Sheep

Horse

Monkey

Dog

Animal Signs Puzzles

Print, cut and start puzzling

SIGNING courses

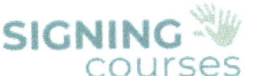

Animal Signs Puzzles

Print, cut and start puzzling

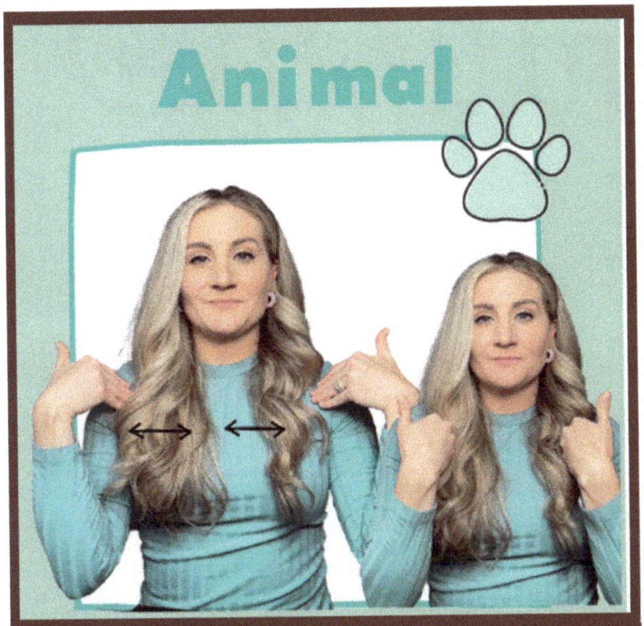

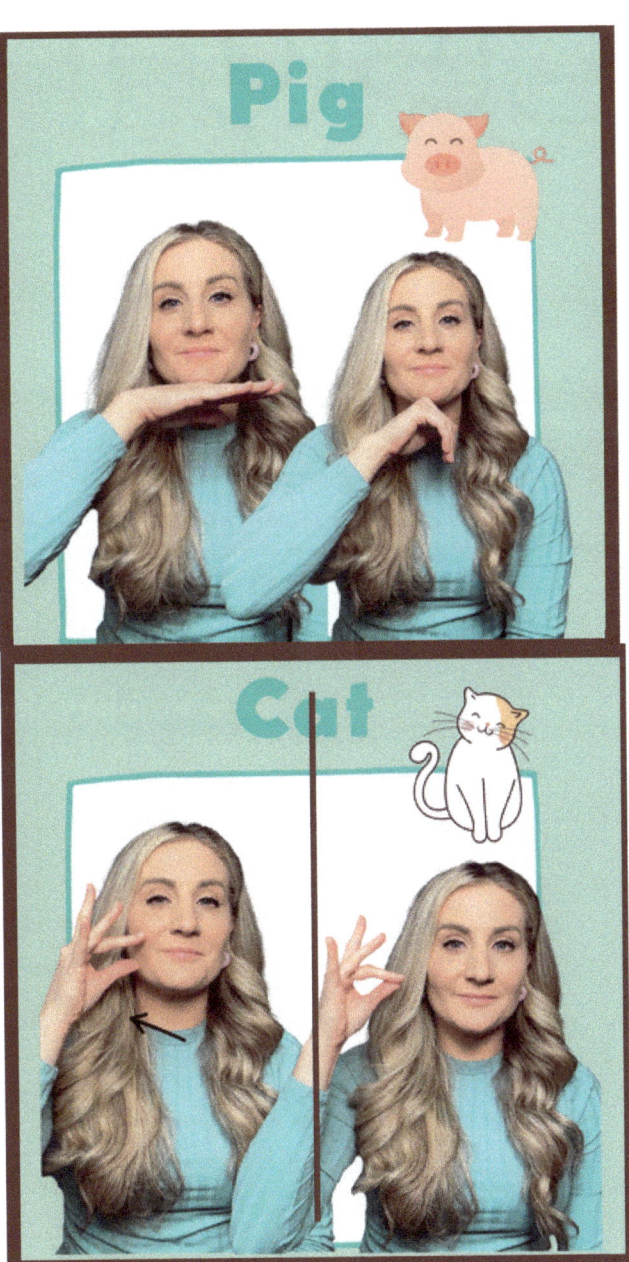

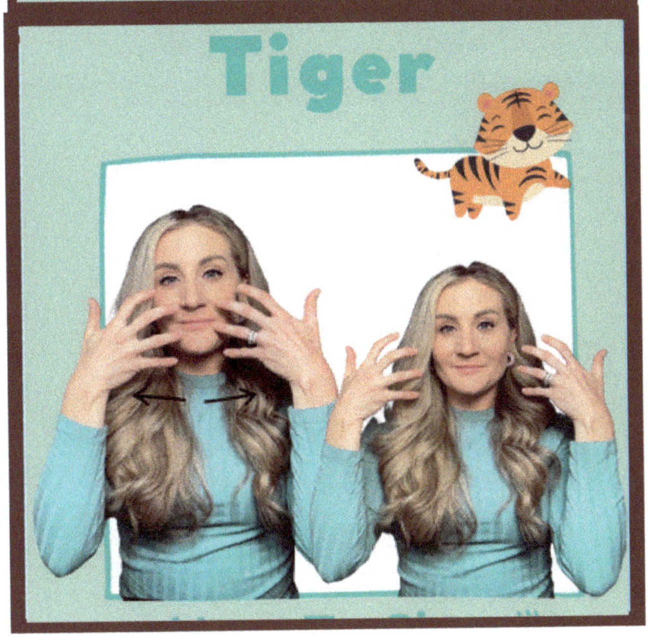

CLOTHING

SIGNS

Sign and color!

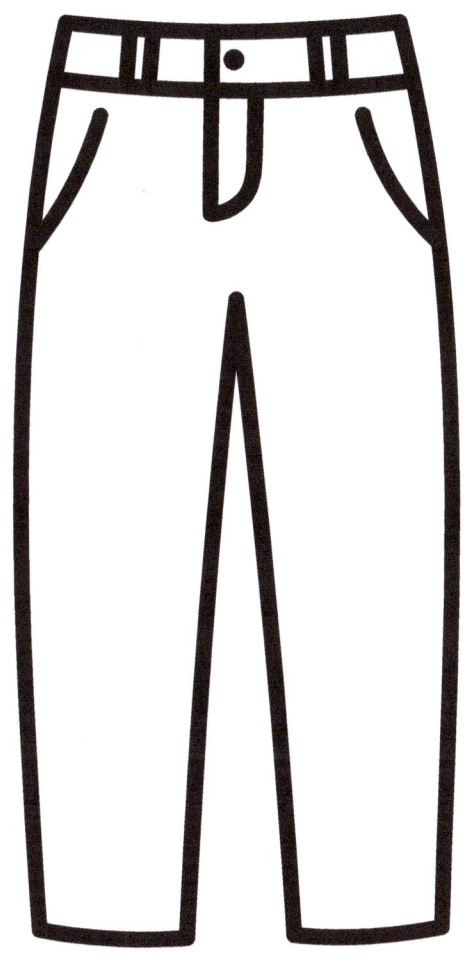

Pants

Sign and color!

Shirt

Sign and color!

PJs

Sign and color!

Dress

Sign and color!

Boots

Sign and color!

Hat

Sign and color!

Coat

Sign and color!

Gloves

Sign and color!

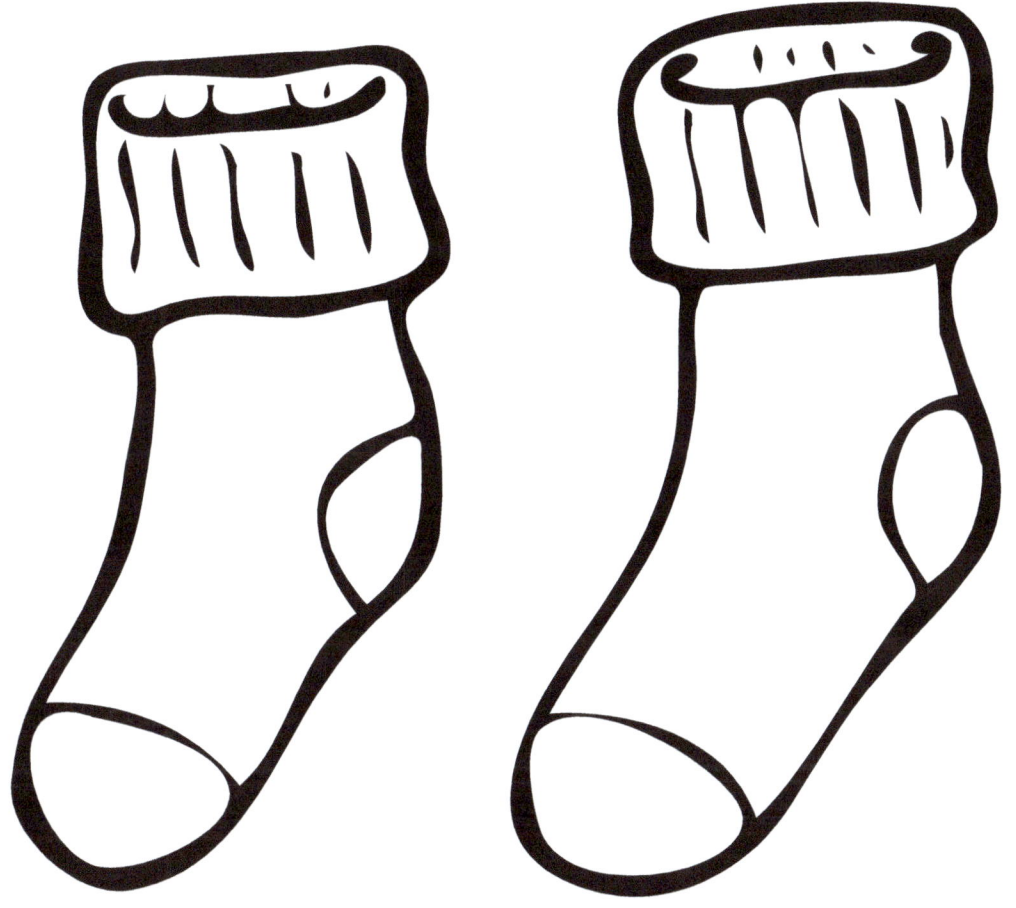

Socks

Sign and color!

Shoes

Sign and color!

Closet

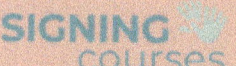

Signing Maze Game

Help the gloves go to the hat.

Gloves

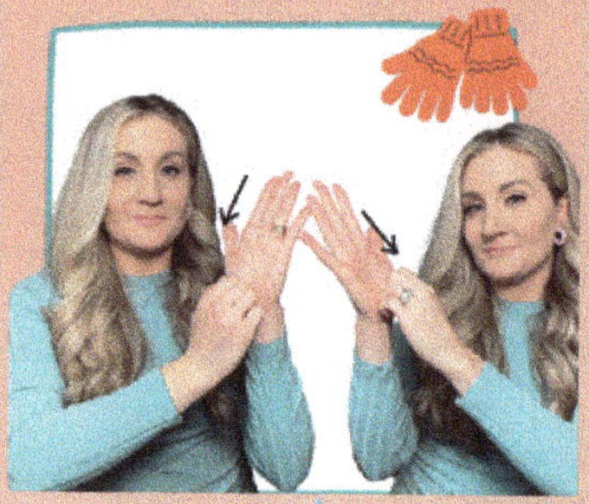

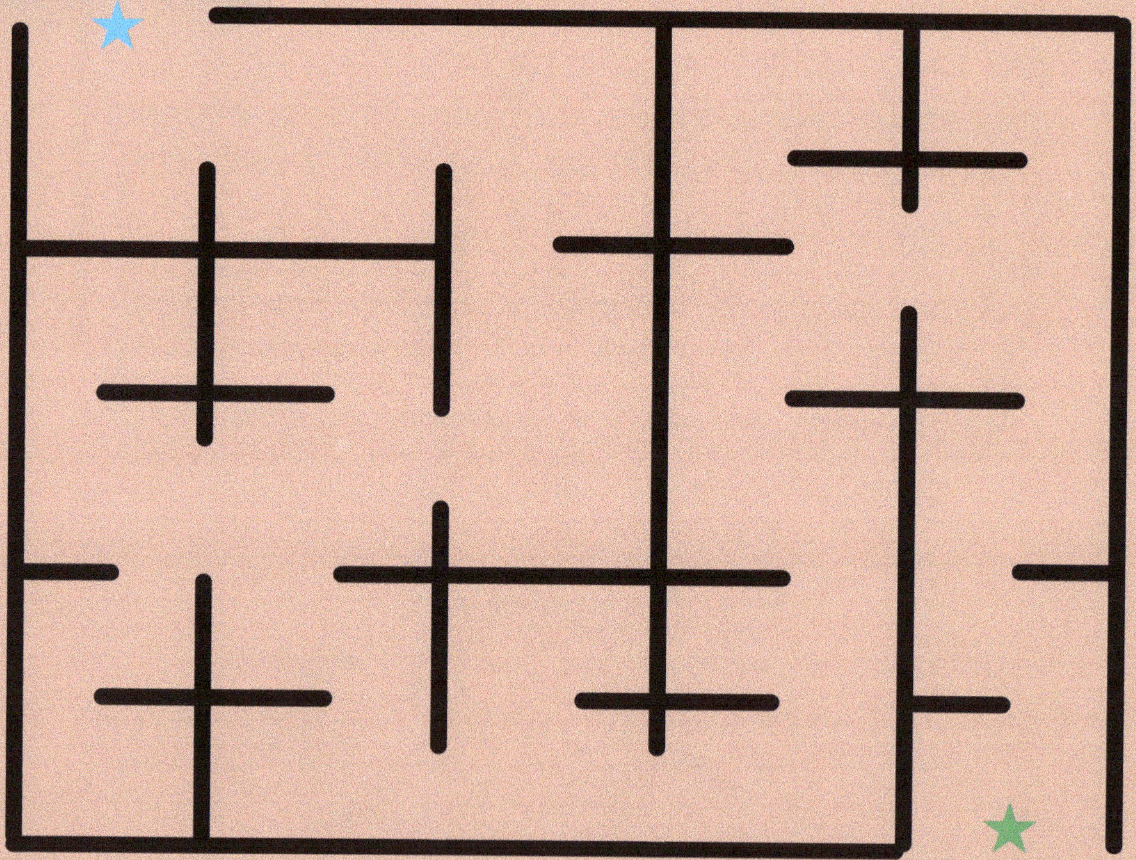

Hat

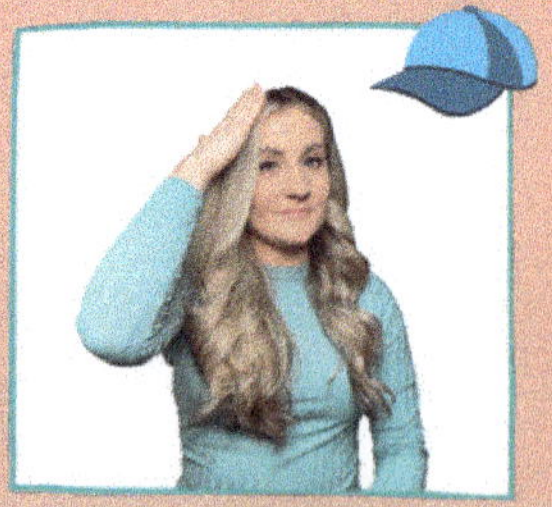

SIGNING courses

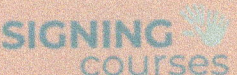

Signing Maze Game

Help the clothes go to the closet.

Clothes

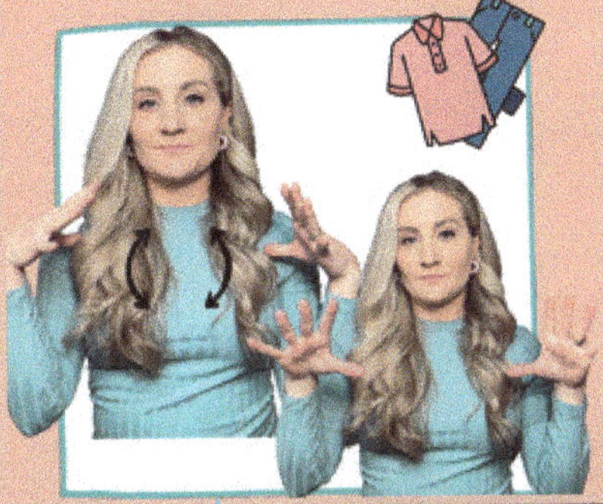

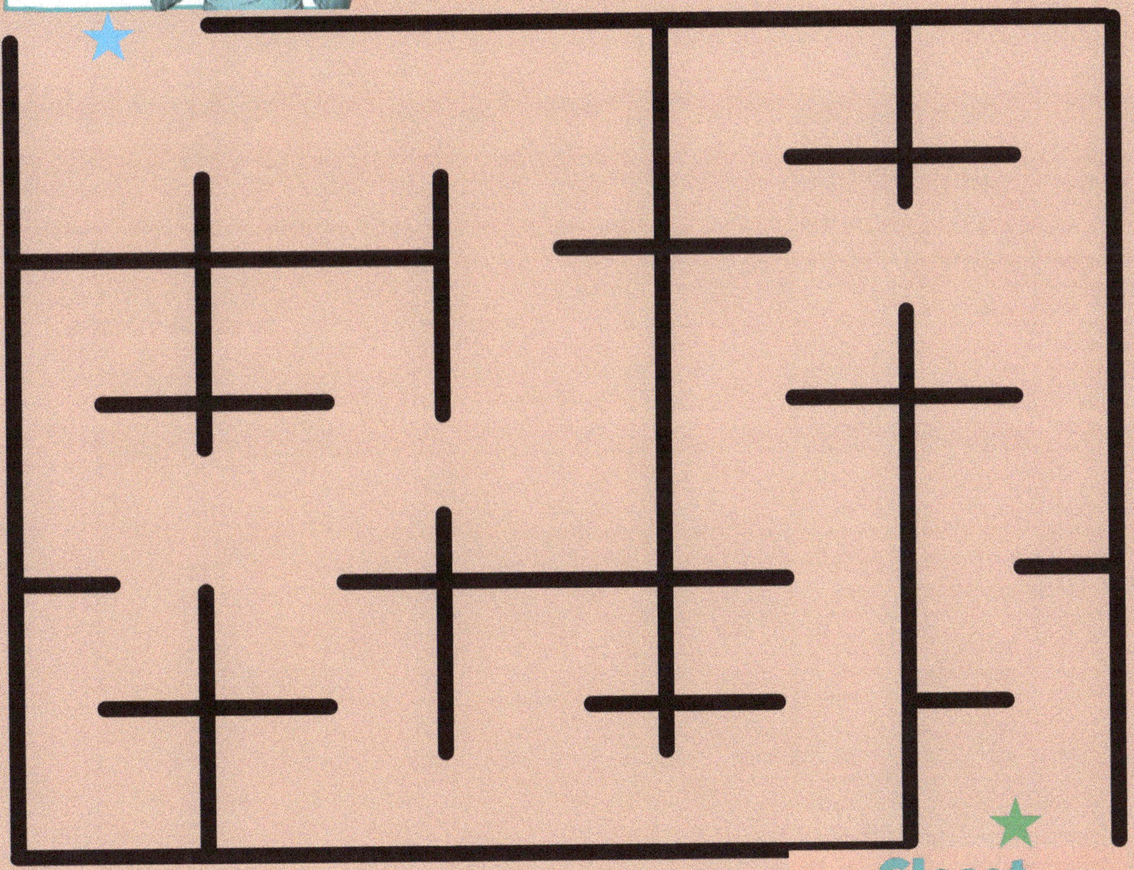

Closet

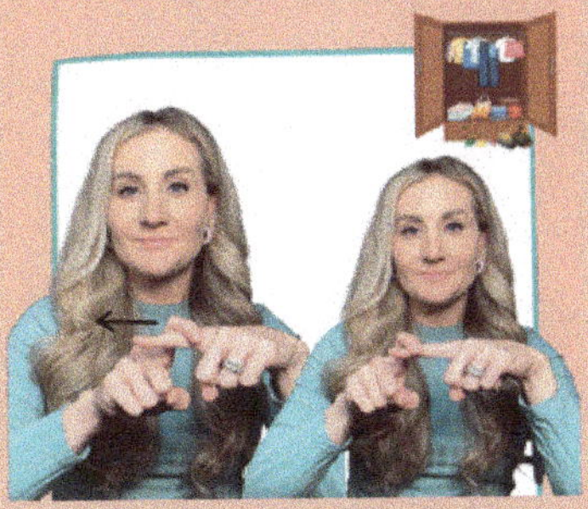

SIGNING courses

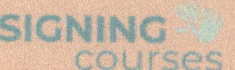

Signing Maze Game

Take the shirt to the pants by following the red car.

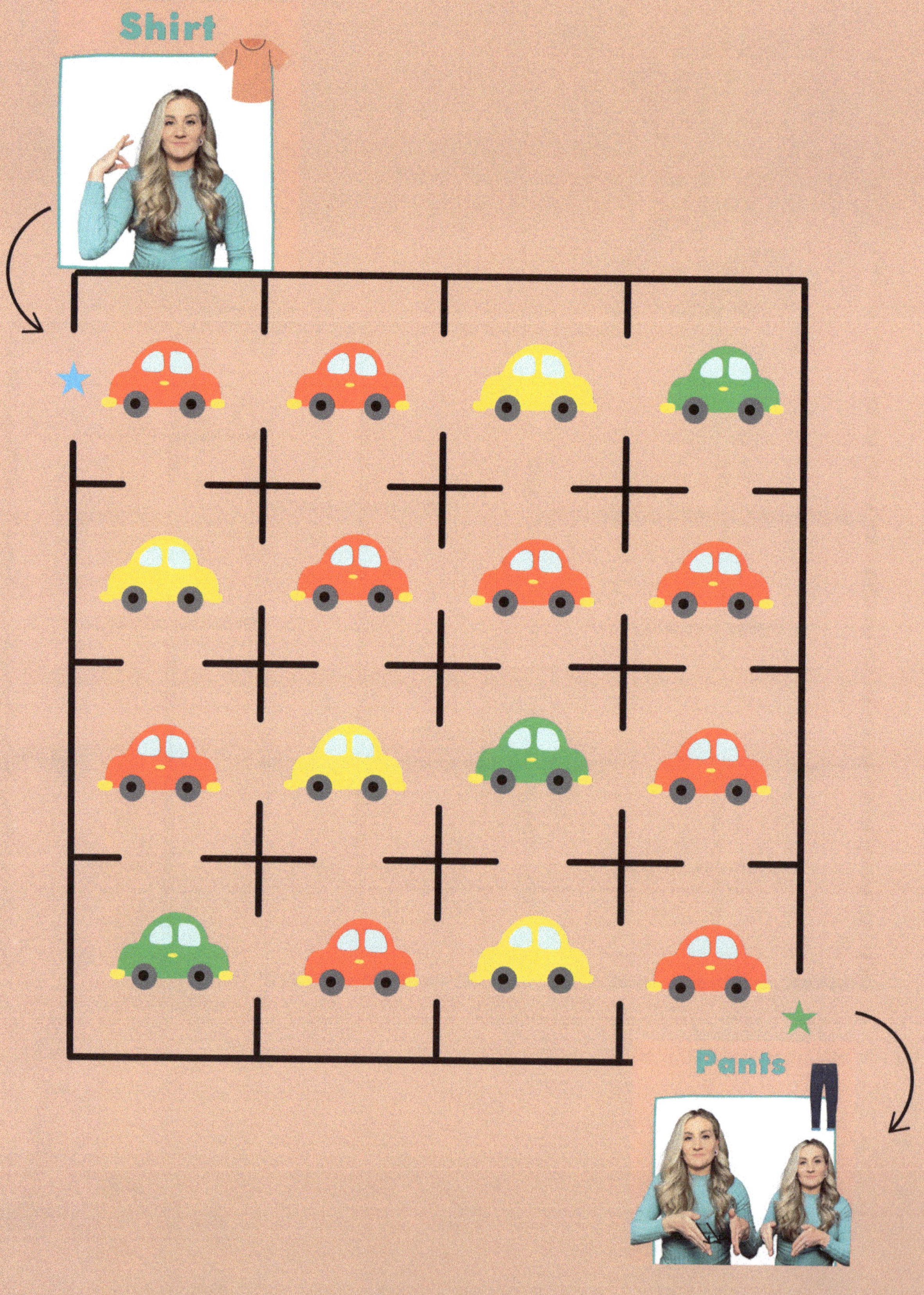

SIGNING courses

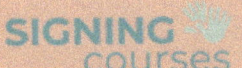

Signing Maze Game

Take the coat to the boots by following the
“I love you” sign

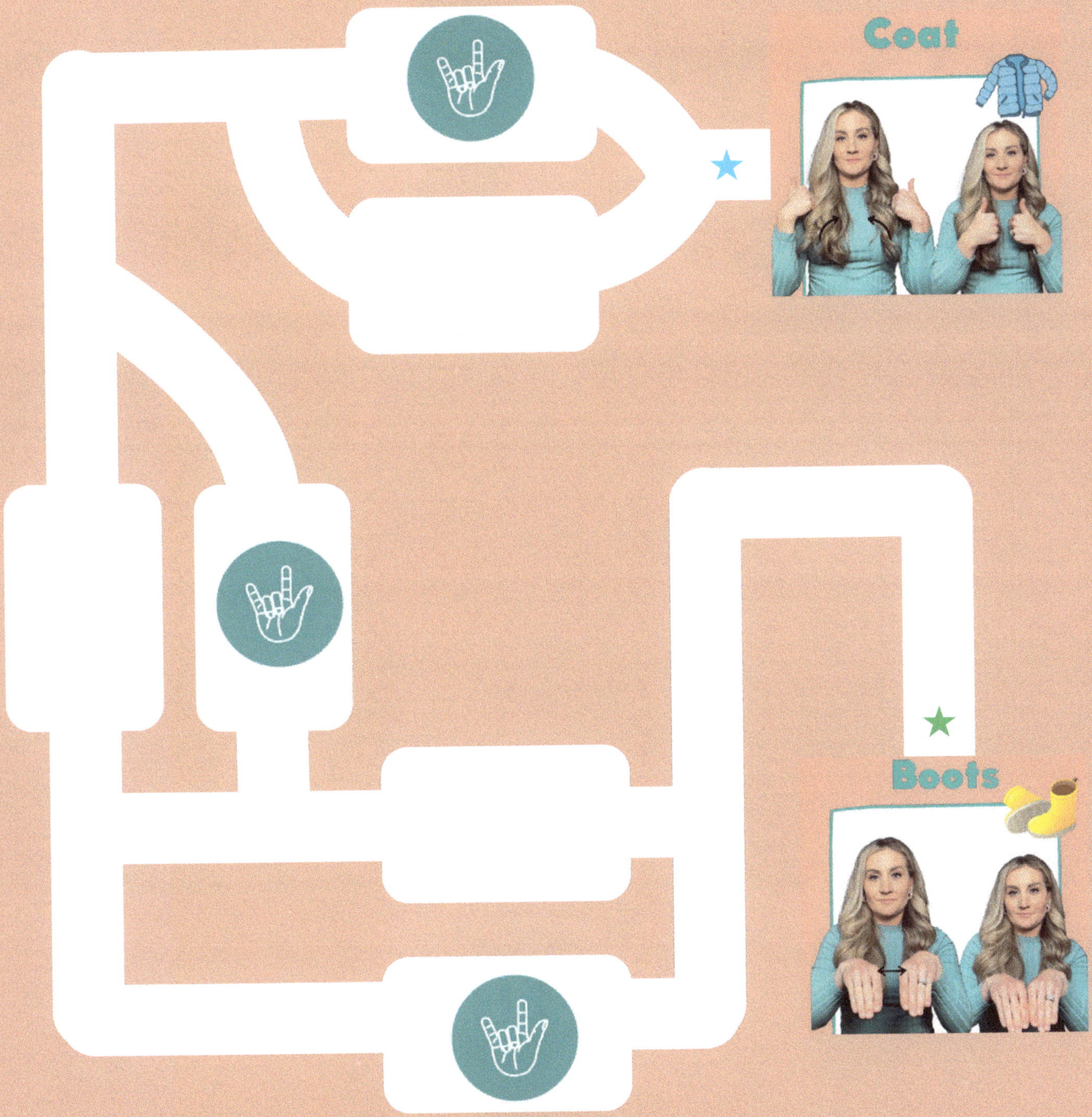

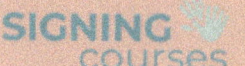

Signing Maze Game

I 'm tired! Dress off, time for PJs. Watch out for the wolf!

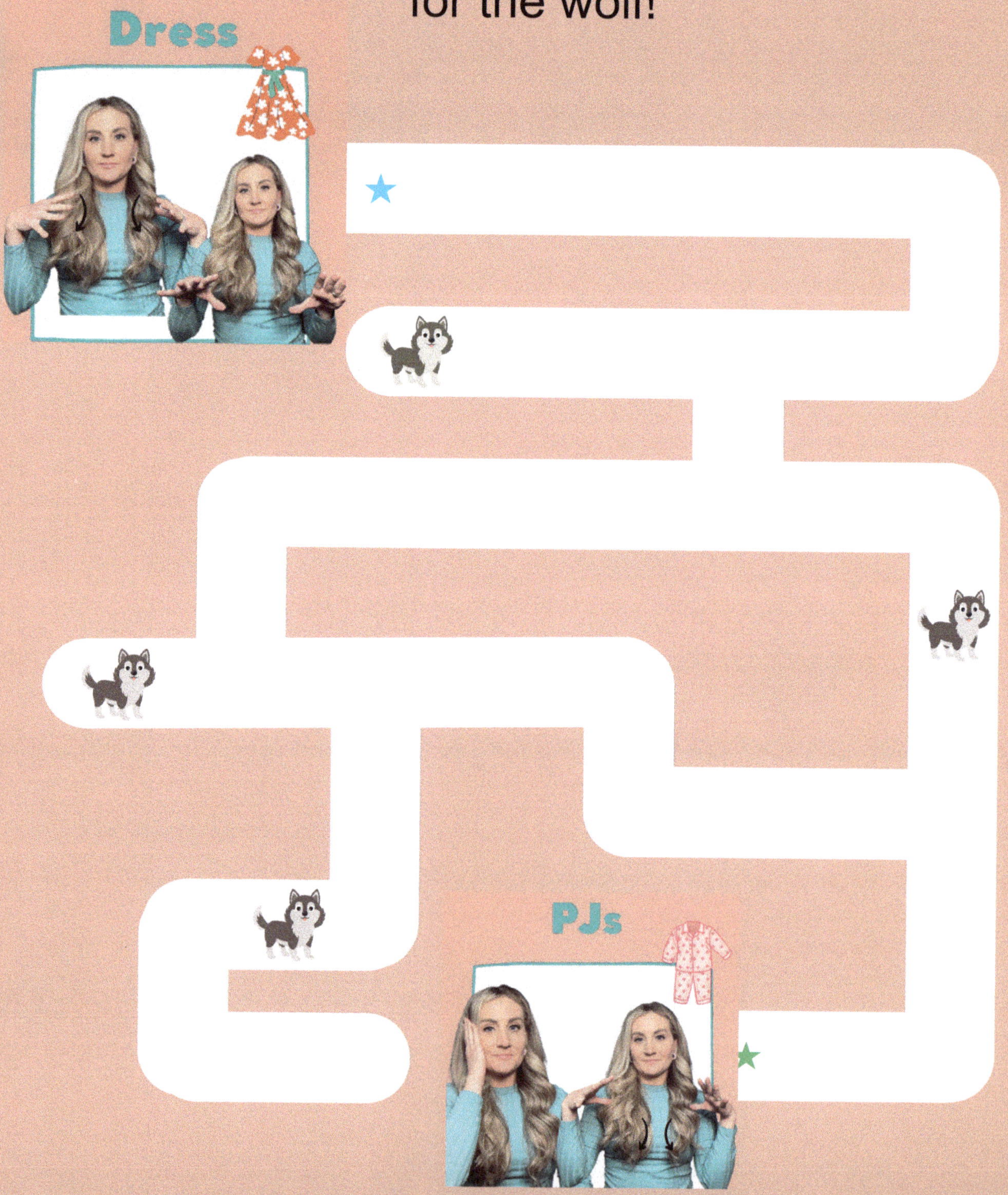

Dress

PJs

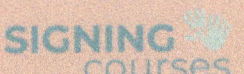
Signing Maze Game

Help the socks go to the shoes.

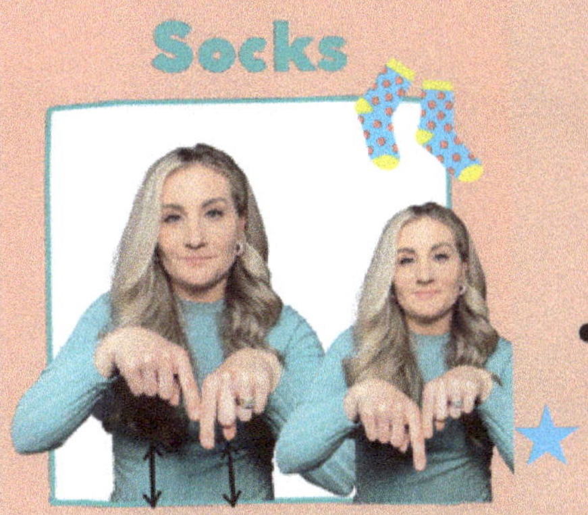

Socks

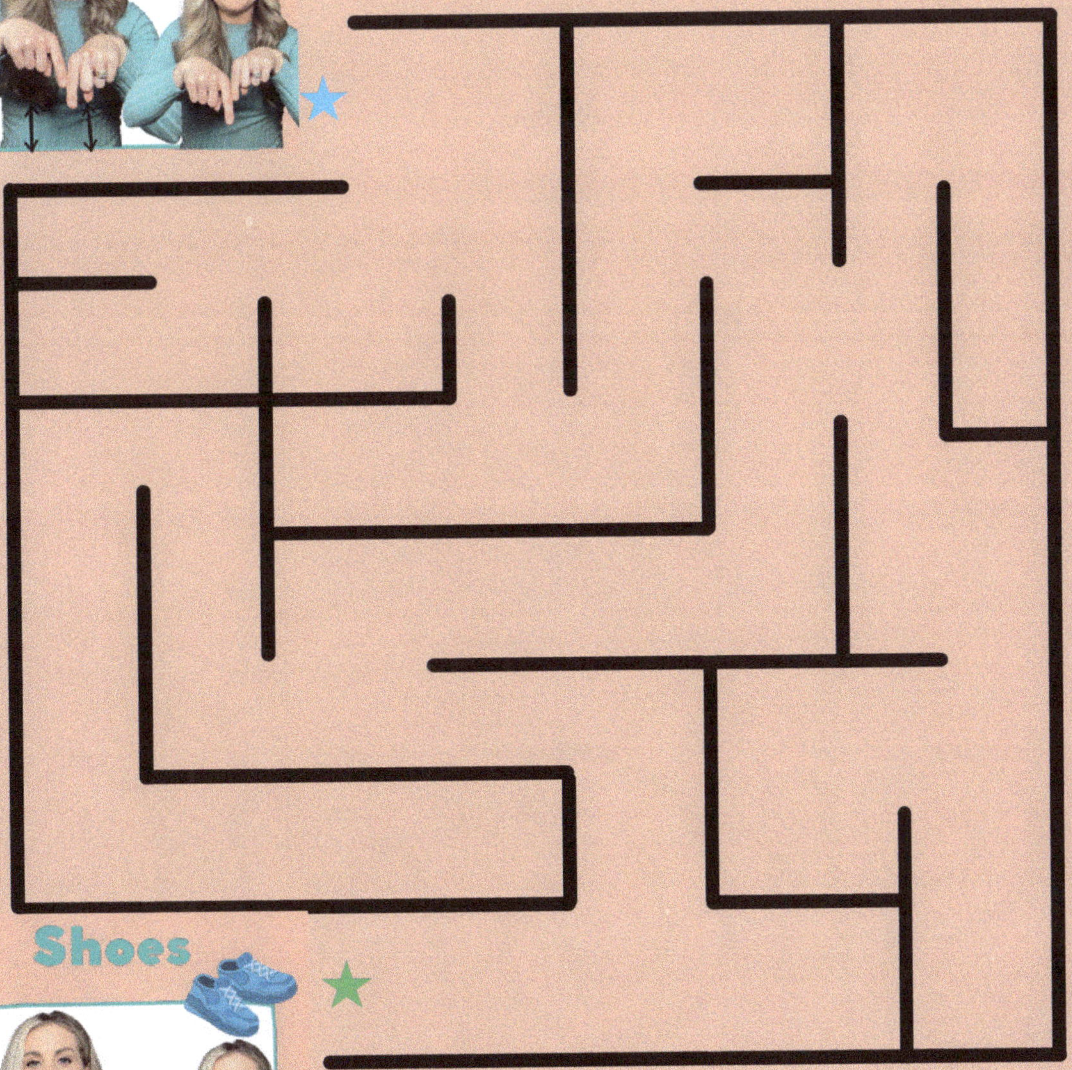

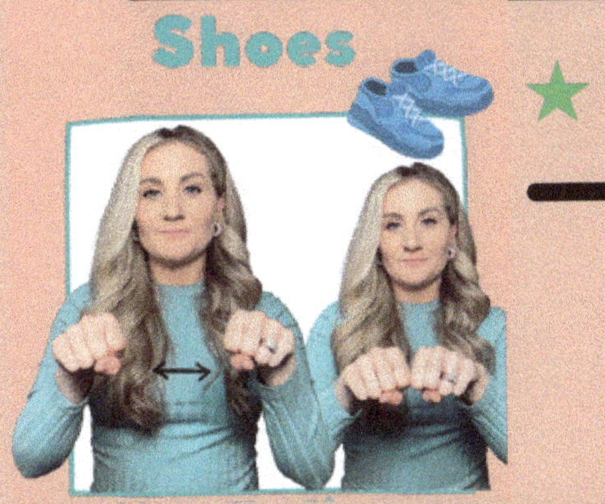

Shoes

FOOD

SIGNS

Sign and color!

Apple

Sign and color!

Sign and color!

Vegetable

Sign and color!

Fruit

Sign and color!

Meat

Sign and color!

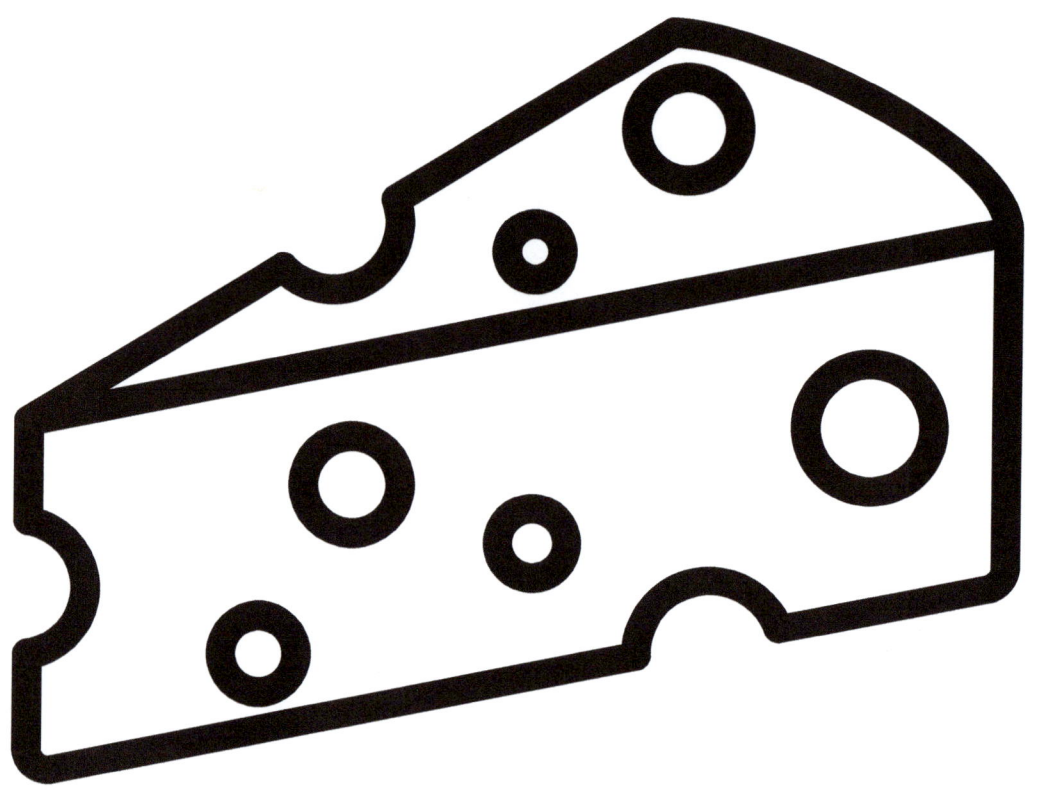

Cheese

Sign and color!

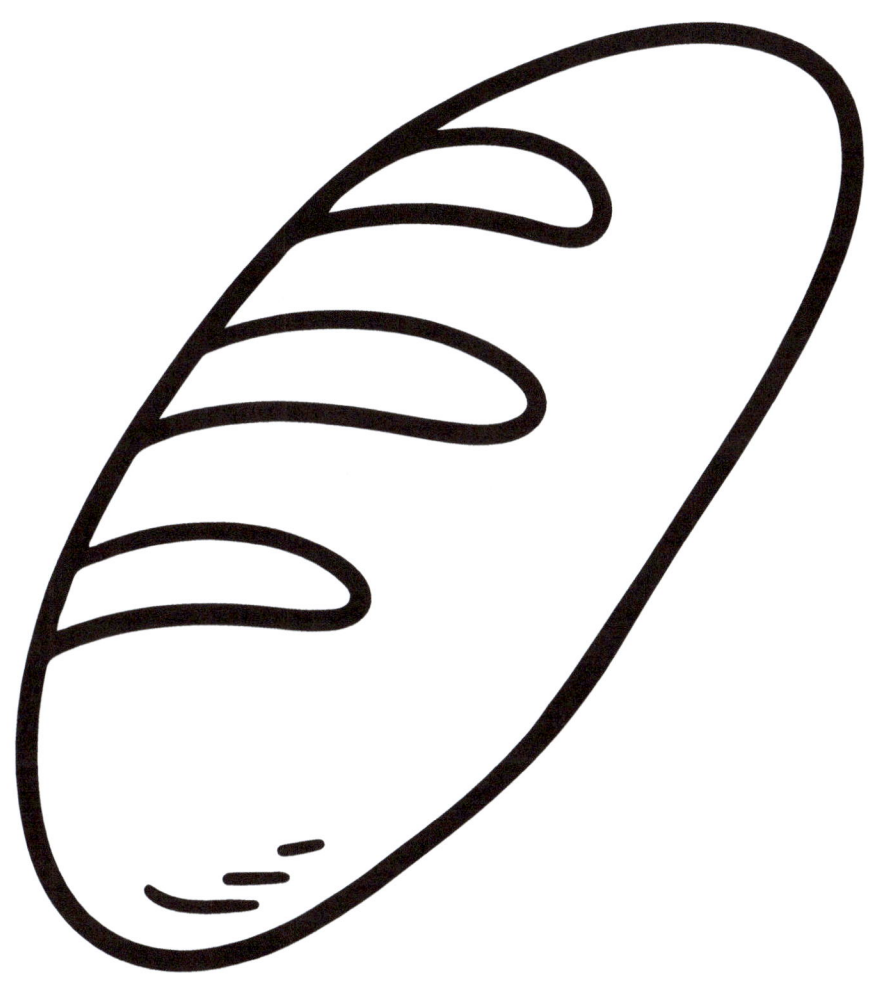

Bread

Sign and color!

Crackers

Sign and color!

Noodles

Sign and color!

Egg

Sign and color!

Cookie

FOOD

What is your favorite food?
Draw it!

WHAT'S THE FOOD?

Match the sign and the word

- Crackers

- Meat

- Fruit

- Noodles

- Vegetable

- Cheese

EMOTIONS

SIGNS

WE ALL EXPERIENCE DIFFERENT EMOTIONS. DRAW WHAT IT LOOKS LIKE TO FEEL SILLY.

WE ALL EXPERIENCE DIFFERENT
EMOTIONS. DRAW WHAT IT LOOKS LIKE
TO FEEL TIRED.

WE ALL EXPERIENCE DIFFERENT EMOTIONS. DRAW WHAT IT LOOKS LIKE TO FEEL HAPPY.

WE ALL EXPERIENCE DIFFERENT EMOTIONS. DRAW WHAT IT LOOKS LIKE TO FEEL SAD.

WE ALL EXPERIENCE DIFFERENT EMOTIONS. DRAW WHAT IT LOOKS LIKE TO FEEL BORED.

WE ALL EXPERIENCE DIFFERENT EMOTIONS. DRAW WHAT IT LOOKS LIKE TO FEEL ANGRY.

WE ALL EXPERIENCE DIFFERENT EMOTIONS. DRAW WHAT IT LOOKS LIKE TO FEEL MOTIVATED/EAGER.

WE ALL EXPERIENCE DIFFERENT EMOTIONS.
DRAW WHAT IT LOOKS LIKE TO FEEL SCARED.

WE ALL EXPERIENCE DIFFERENT EMOTIONS. DRAW WHAT IT LOOKS LIKE TO FEEL FRUSTRATED.

WE ALL EXPERIENCE DIFFERENT EMOTIONS. DRAW WHAT IT LOOKS LIKE TO FEEL SHY.

Shy

WE ALL EXPERIENCE DIFFERENT EMOTIONS. DRAW WHAT IT LOOKS LIKE TO FEEL CONFUSED.

WE ALL EXPERIENCE DIFFERENT EMOTIONS.
DRAW WHAT IT LOOKS LIKE TO FEEL LOVE.

SIGNING courses

Instructions : Cut out calling cards and place in a bag or container. Draw out one card at a time and students will mark off their bingo board with a counter or marker.

Love 	Confused 	Shy 
Frustrated 	Scared 	Bored 
Sad 	Angry 	Motivated/Eager 

Instructions : Cut out calling cards and place in a bag or container. Draw out one card at a time and students will mark off their bingo board with a counter or marker.

BINGO

Happy	Tired	Bored

Sad		Angry
	FREE	

Frustrated	Motivated/Eager	Scared

SIGNING courses

BINGO

Sad 	Angry 	Motivated/Eager 
Happy 	FREE	Tired 
Scared 	Silly 	Frustrated 

BINGO

Happy 	**Tired** 	**Confused** 
Love 	FREE	**Angry** 
Frustrated 	**Shy** 	**Scared** 

BINGO

Happy 	**Tired** 	**Confused** 
Love 	FREE	**Angry** 
Frustrated 	**Shy** 	**Scared** 

BINGO

Scared	Tired	Bored

Love 	FREE	**Sad** 
Motivated/Eager 	**Confused** 	**Frustrated** 

BINGO

Confused 	**Silly** 	**Frustrated** 
Scared 	FREE	**Tired** 
Shy 	**Bored** 	**Happy** 

WEATHER

SIGNS

Sign and color!

Cold/Winter

Sign and color!

Fall

Sign and color!

Sign and color!

Hot

Sign and color!

Spring

Sign and color!

Sign and color!

Snow

Sign and color!

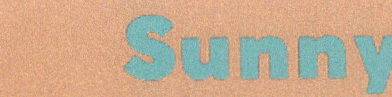

Sign and color!

Windy

Sign and color!

Cloudy

Sign and color!

Season

WEATHER TRACING

Trace the lines and color the picture.

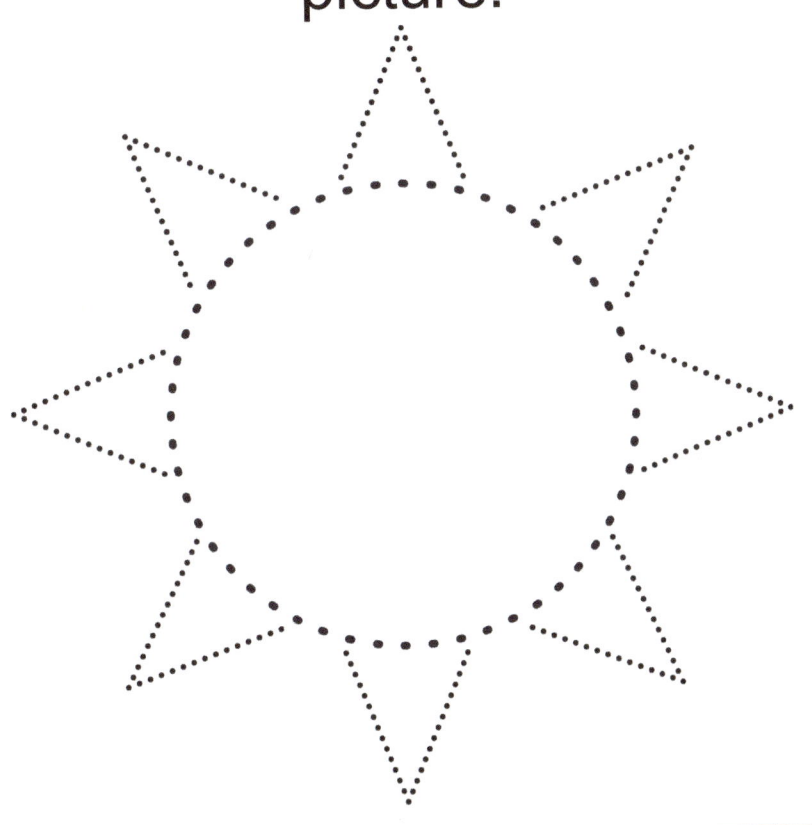

Sunny

WEATHER TRACING

Trace the lines and color the picture.

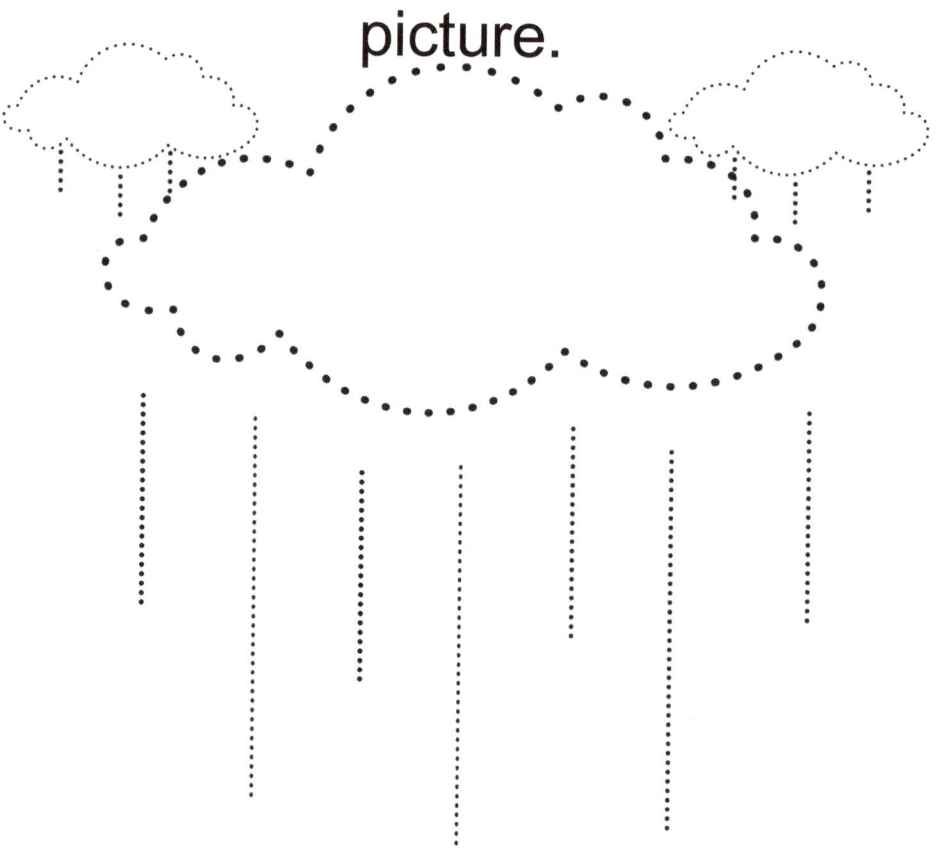

WEATHER TRACING

Trace the lines and color the picture.

Cloudy

WEATHER TRACING

Trace the lines and color the picture.

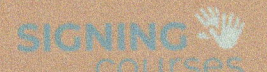

CUTTING OR TEARING PRACTICE

Use scissors to carefully cut along the lines or tear the paper.

SPRING   FALL WINTER SUMMER

WHAT'S THE WEATHER?

Match the sign and the word

Cold/Winter

•   • Sunny

Snow

•   • Cloudy

Rain

•   • Cold/winter

Windy

•   • Snowy

Sunny

•   • Rainy

Cloudy

•   • Windy

WHAT'S THE WEATHER?

Attach the arrow using a pin.
Spin it and then tell what the weather is today.

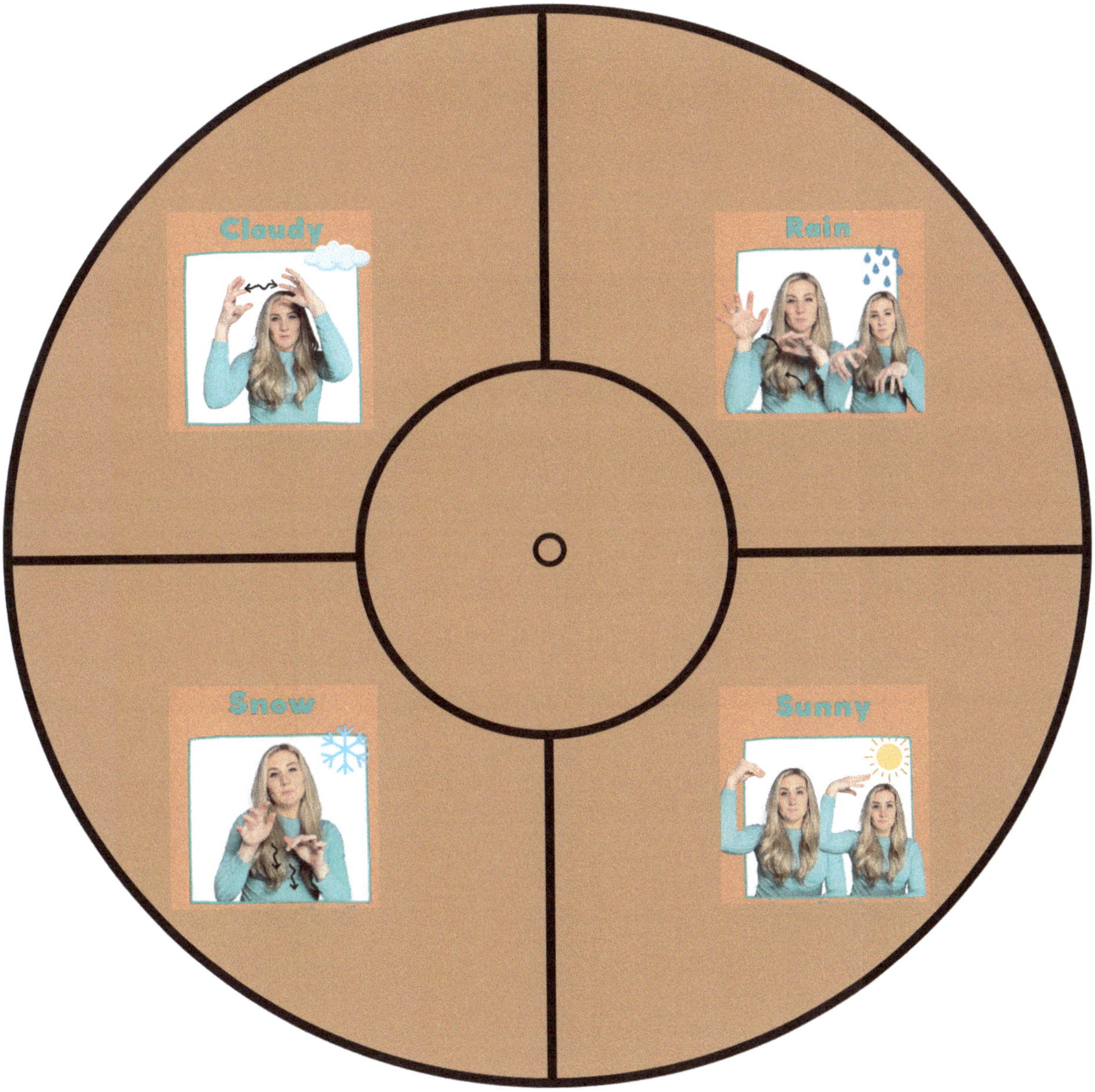

Weekly Weather Record

Weather signs:

Day	Temperature	Rainfall	Weather
MON			
TUES			
WED			
THUR			
FRI			

WEATHER

What is your favorite weather?
Draw it!

FAMILY

SIGNS

Draw what a family looks like to you.

Draw what a mom looks like to you.

Draw what a dad looks like to you.

Father/Dad

Draw what a grandma looks like to you.

Draw what a grandpa looks like to you.

Draw what an uncle looks like to you.

Draw what an aunt looks like to you.

Aunt

Draw what a sister looks like to you.

Draw what a brother looks like to you.

Draw what a cousin looks like to you.

Draw what a baby looks like to you.

Baby

Draw what home looks like to you.

Home

Instructions : Cut out calling cards and place in a bag or container. Draw out one card at a time and students will mark off their bingo board with a counter or marker.

Instructions : Cut out calling cards and place in a bag or container. Draw out one card at a time and students will mark off their bingo board with a counter or marker.

BINGO

Family	Father/Dad	Mother/Mom

Sister	FREE	Aunt

Uncle	Grandpa	Grandma

BINGO

Family 	**Father/Dad** 	**Mother/Mom** 
Sister 	FREE	**Aunt** 
Uncle 	**Grandpa** 	**Grandma** 

BINGO

Uncle	Family	Grandma

Home	FREE	Mother/Mom

Cousin	Father/Dad	Sister

BINGO

Baby	Brother	Grandma

Sister 	FREE	**Aunt** 
Mother/Mom 	**Home** 	**Grandpa** 

SIGNING courses
BINGO

Grandma	Sister	Family

Baby 	FREE	**Grandpa** 
Father/Dad 	**Aunt** 	**Home** 

BINGO

Father/Dad	Cousin	Home

Aunt	FREE	Family

Sister	Grandpa	Baby

CUTTING OR TEARING PRACTICE

Use scissors to carefully cut along the lines or tear the paper.

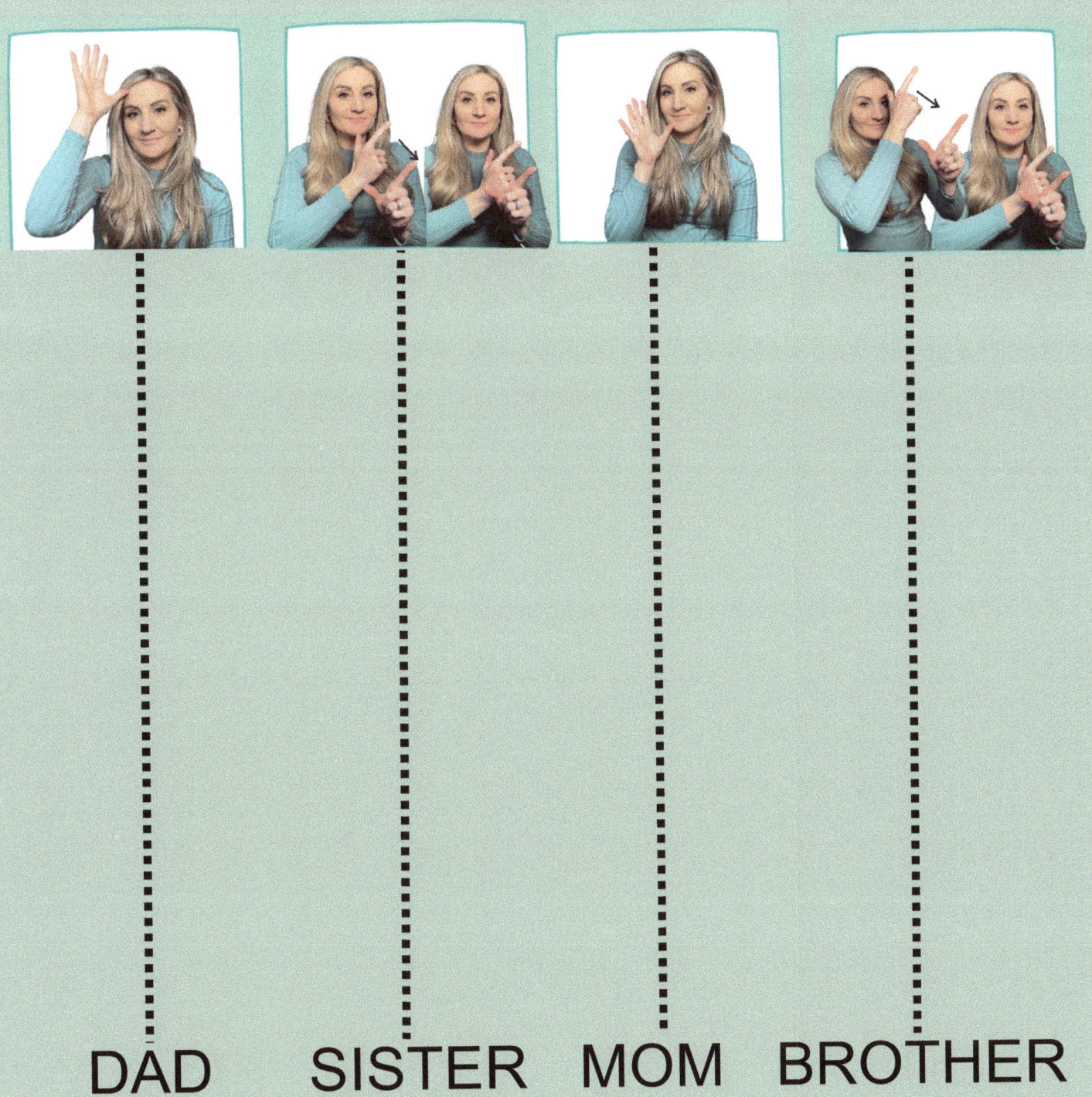

DAD   SISTER   MOM   BROTHER

CUTTING OR TEARING PRACTICE

Use scissors to carefully cut along the lines or tear the paper.

COUSIN   BABY   HOME   FAMILY

HEALTH

SIGNS

Sign and color!

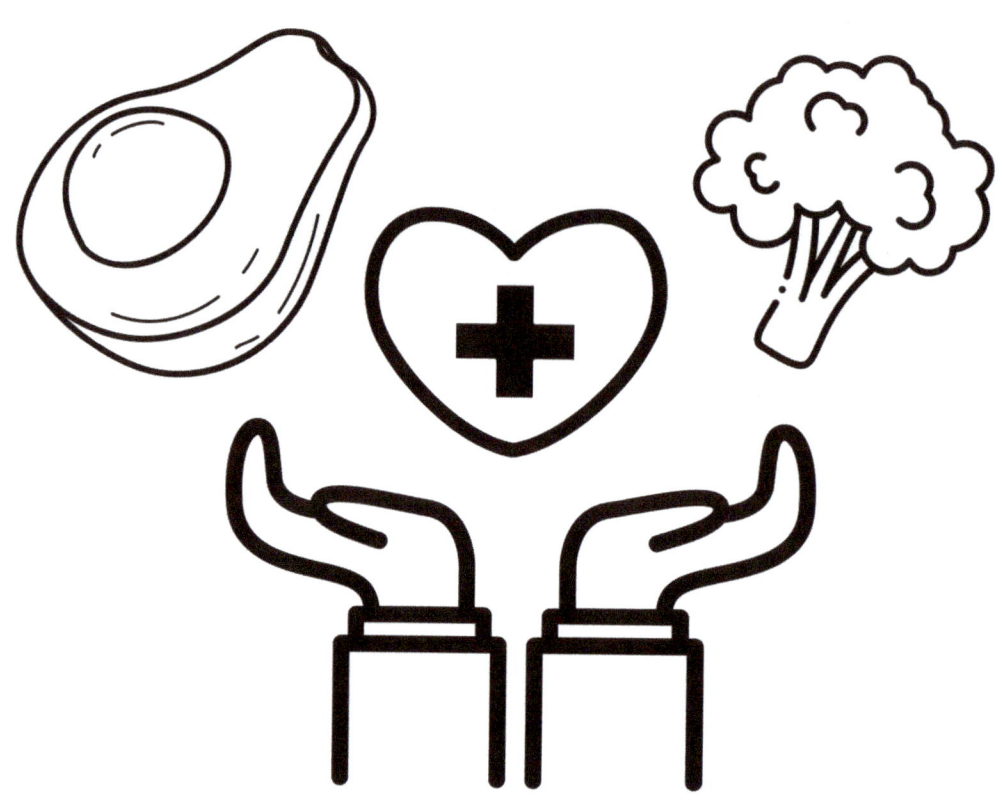

Sign and color!

Fever

Sign and color!

Queasy/Nauseous

Sign and color!

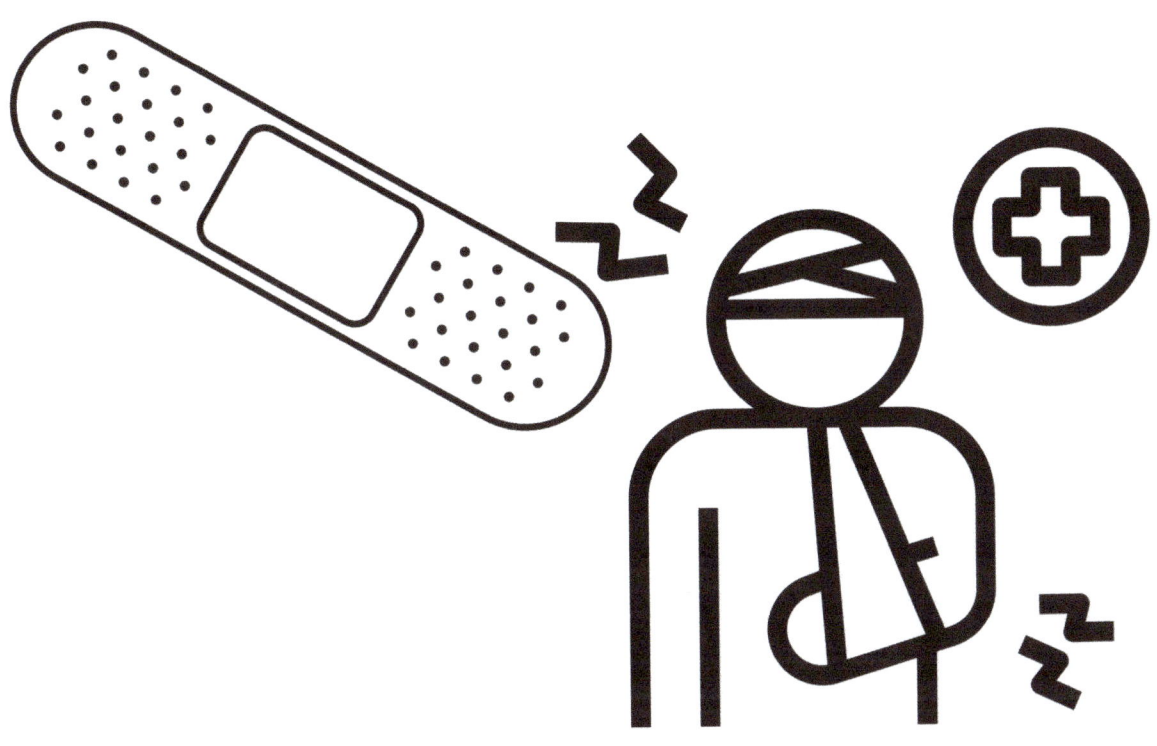

Hurt

Sign and color!

Sign and color!

Doctor & Medicine

Sign and color!

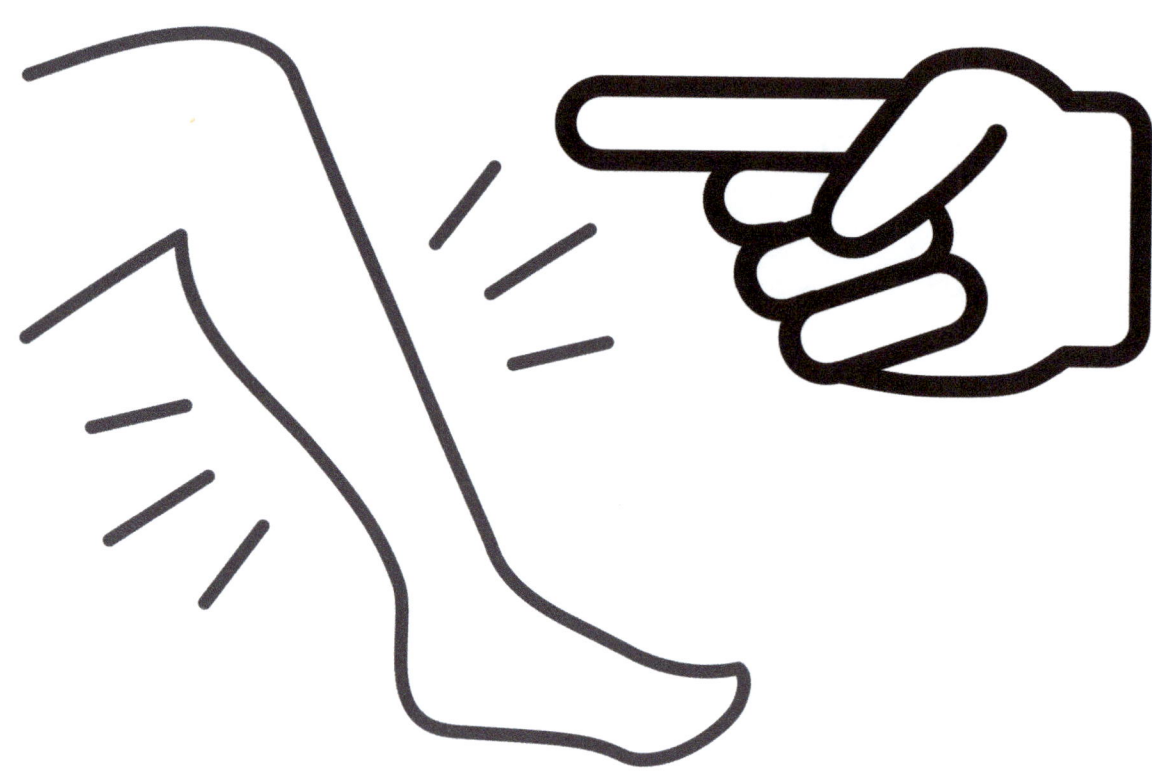

Sign and color!

Better

Sign and color!

Sign and color!

Headache

Sign and color!

Runny Nose

Sign and color!

Sick

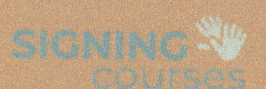

WHAT'S THE SIGN?

Match the sign and the word

Doctor & Medicine

- •   • Sick

Sick

- •   • Runny Nose

Queasy/Nauseous

- •   • Doctor/ Medicine

Health/Healthy

- •   • Cough

Cough

- •   • Nauseous/ Queasy

Runny Nose

- •   • Health/ Healthy

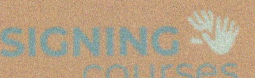

Signing Maze Game

Take the sign for sick to the doctor by following the "I love you" sign

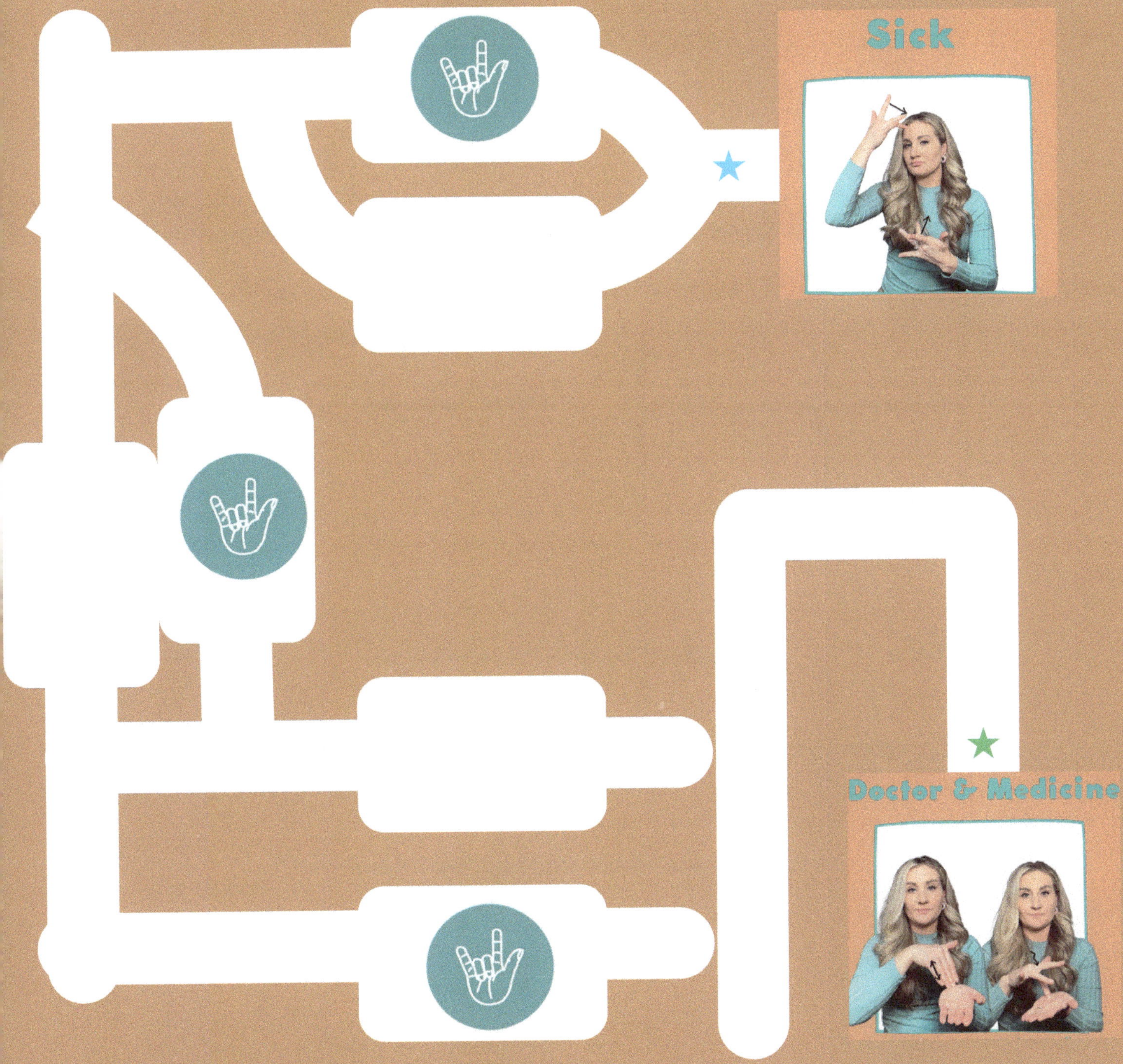

Sick

Doctor & Medicine

Signing Maze Game

Help the headache sign get to the better sign.

Headache

Better

THE ALPHABET

A B C

Apple

B b

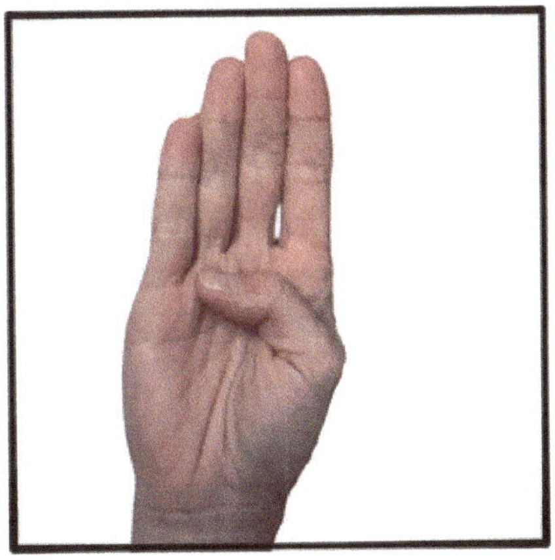

Ball

C c

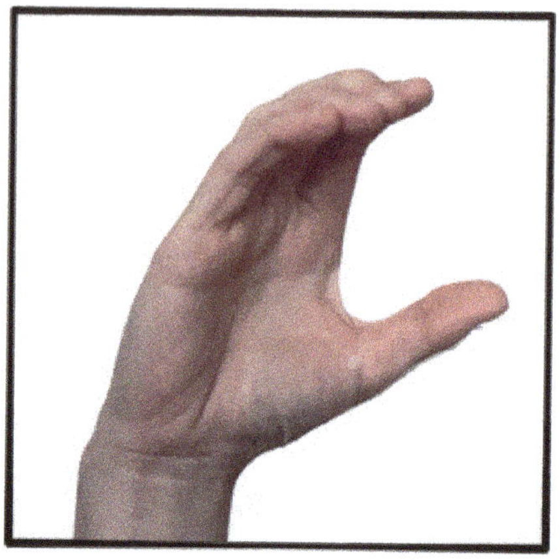

Cake

Dd

Donut

E e

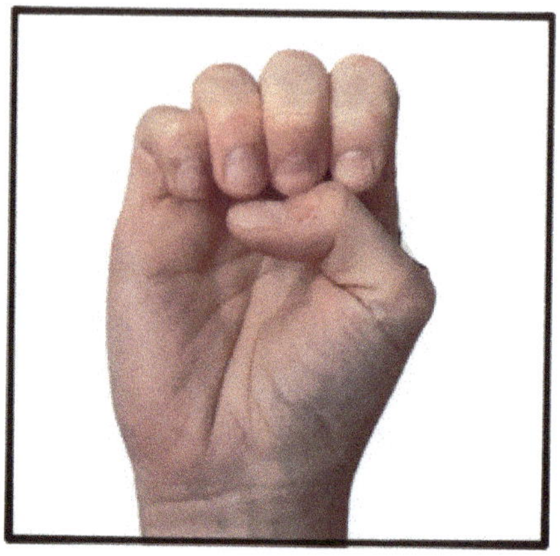

Elephant

F f

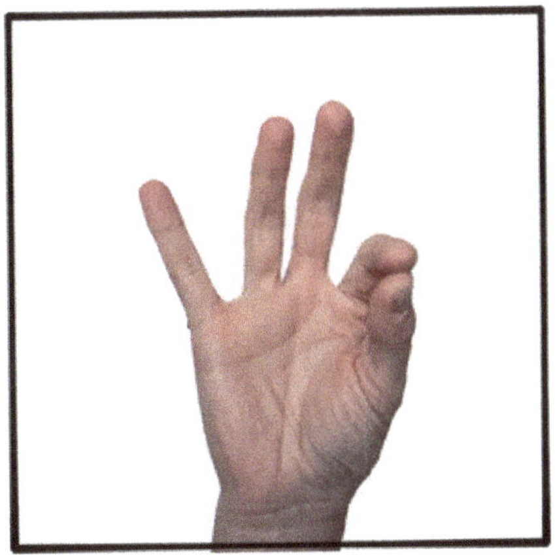

Fire

Gg

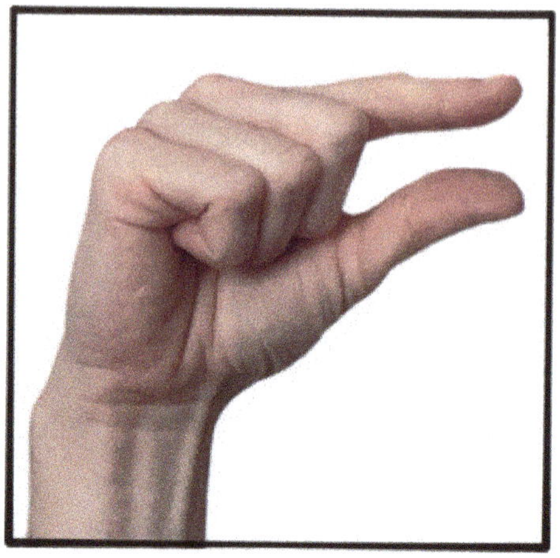

Guitar

 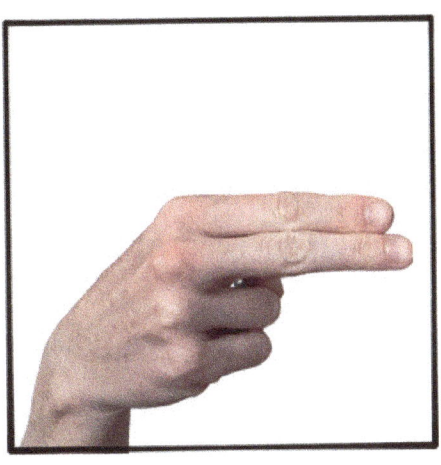

Hat

Ice cream

J j

Draw a J with your pinky

Juice

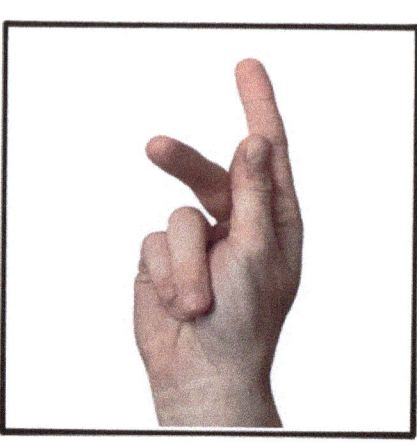

Kite

SIGNING courses

Ll

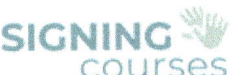

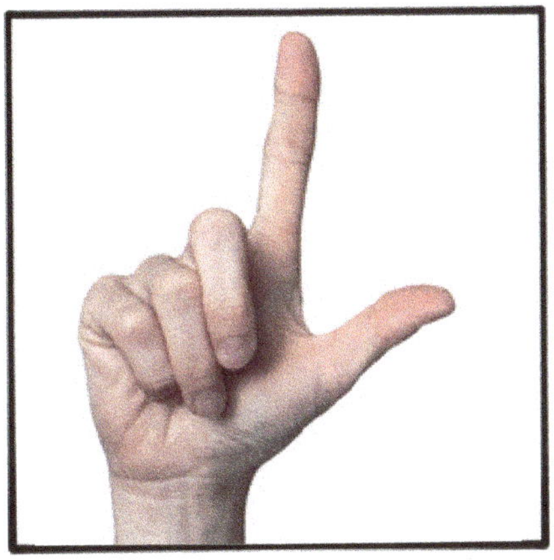

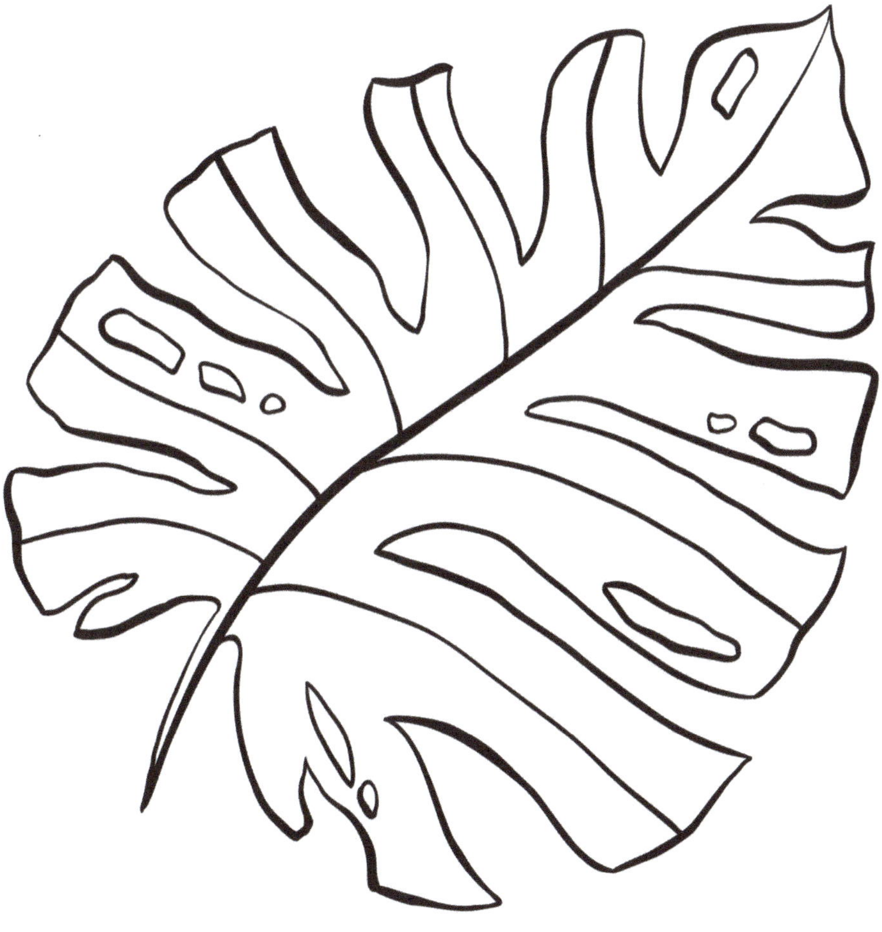

Leaf

SIGNING courses

Mm

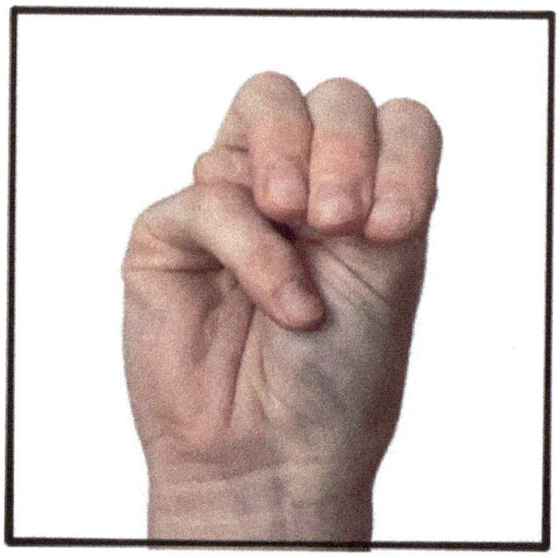

MILK
L

Milk

Nn

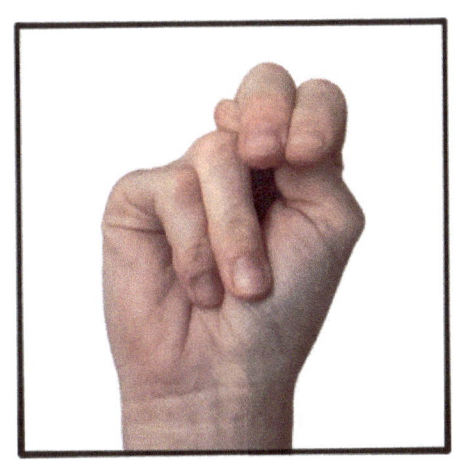

Nurse

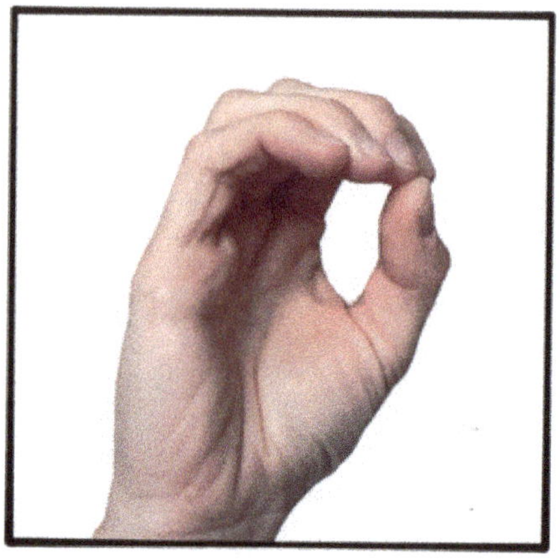

Octopus

P p

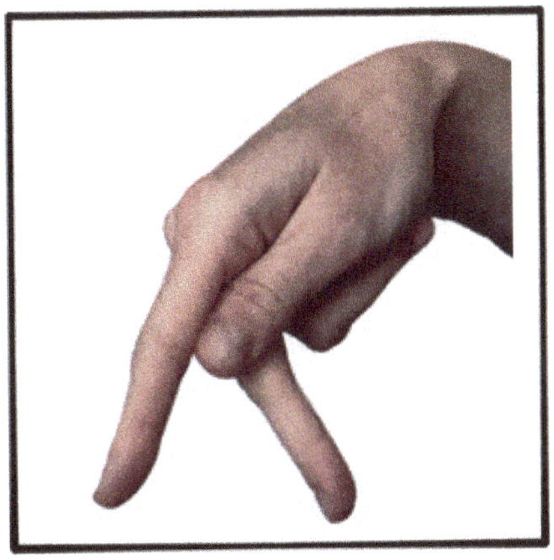

Pizza

SIGNING courses

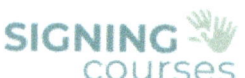

Qq

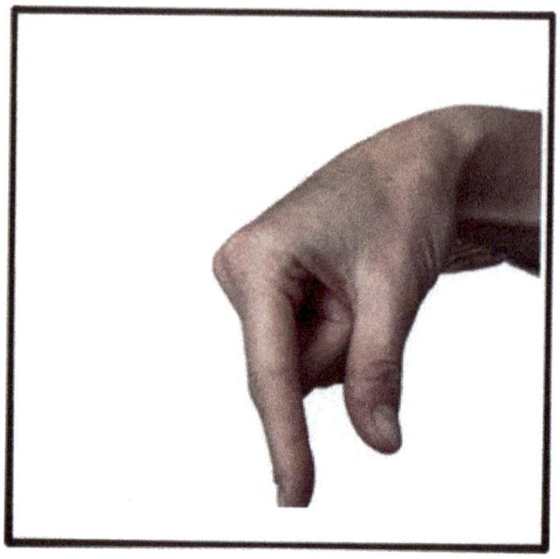

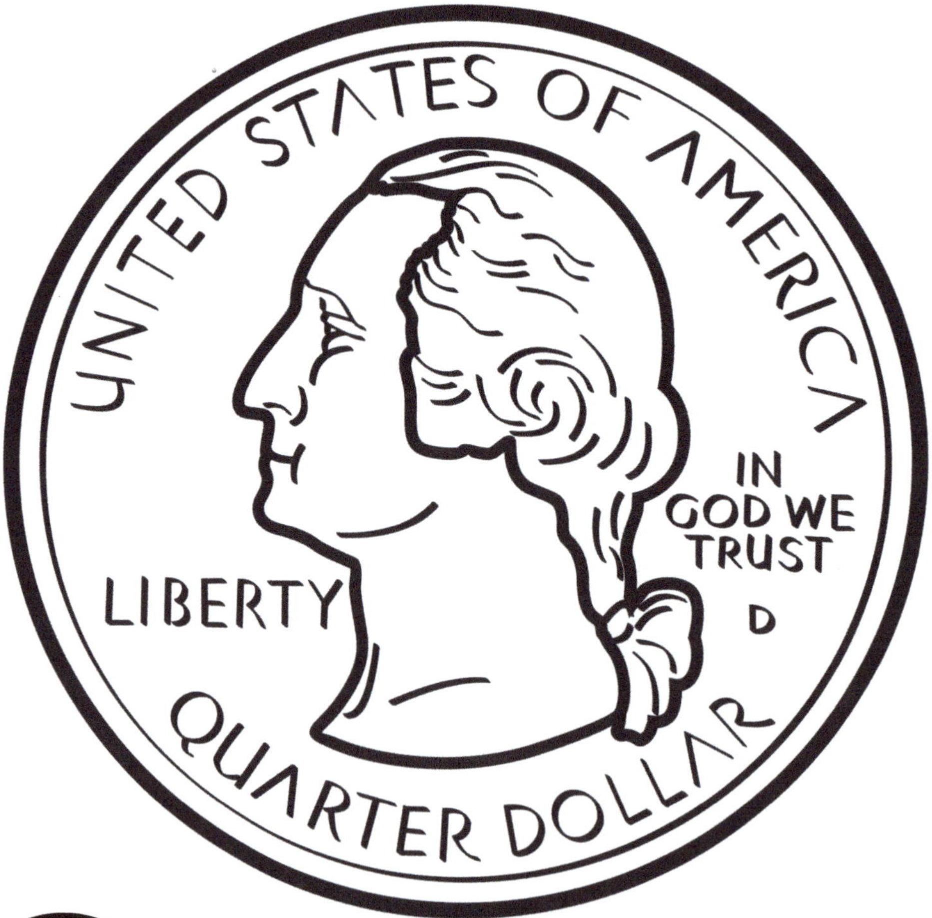
UNITED STATES OF AMERICA
IN GOD WE TRUST
LIBERTY
D
QUARTER DOLLAR

Quarter

Rr

Rocket

S s

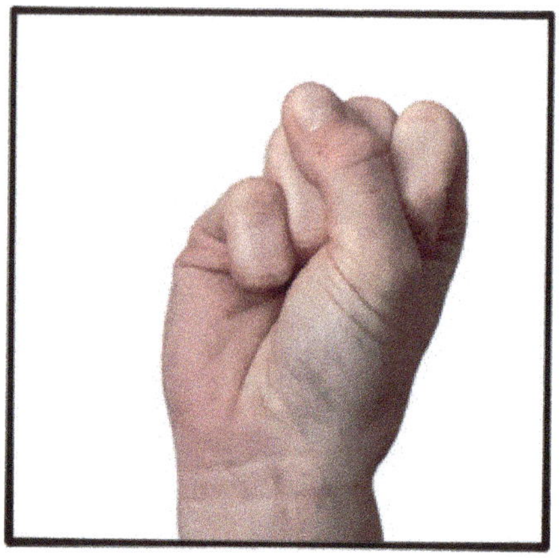

Sun

T t

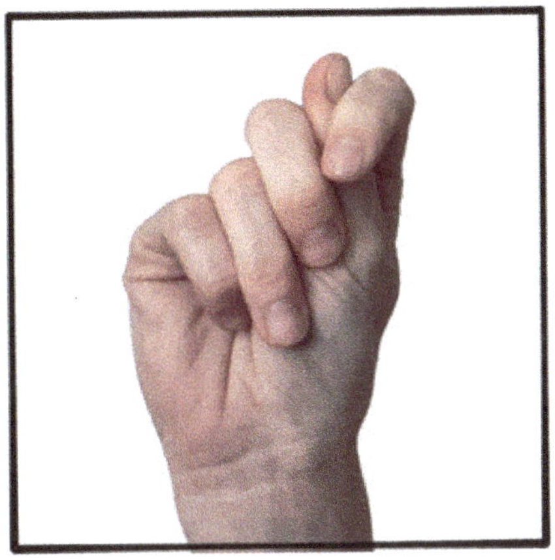

Tree

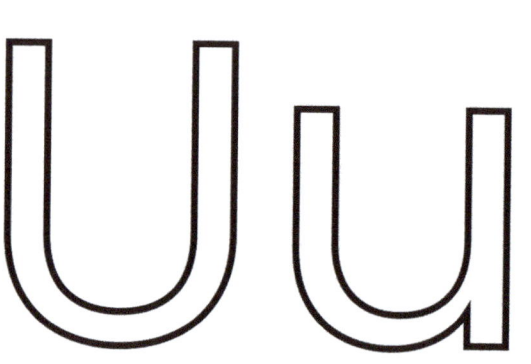

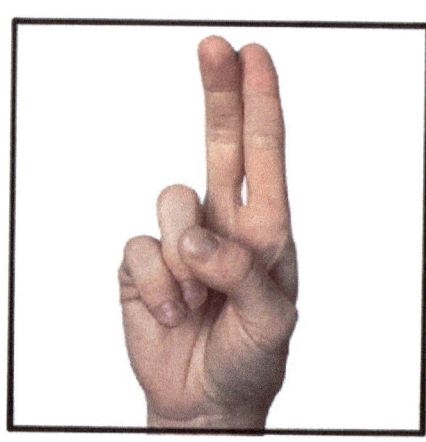

Umbrella

Vv

Violin

Ww

Watch

X x

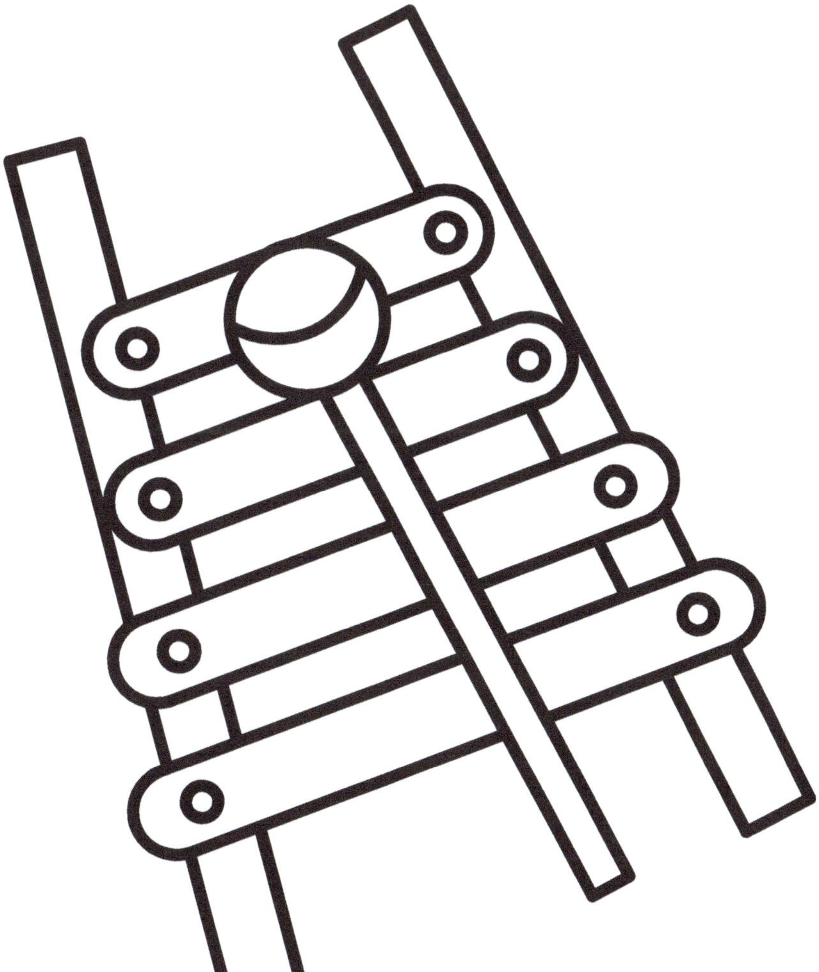

Xylophone

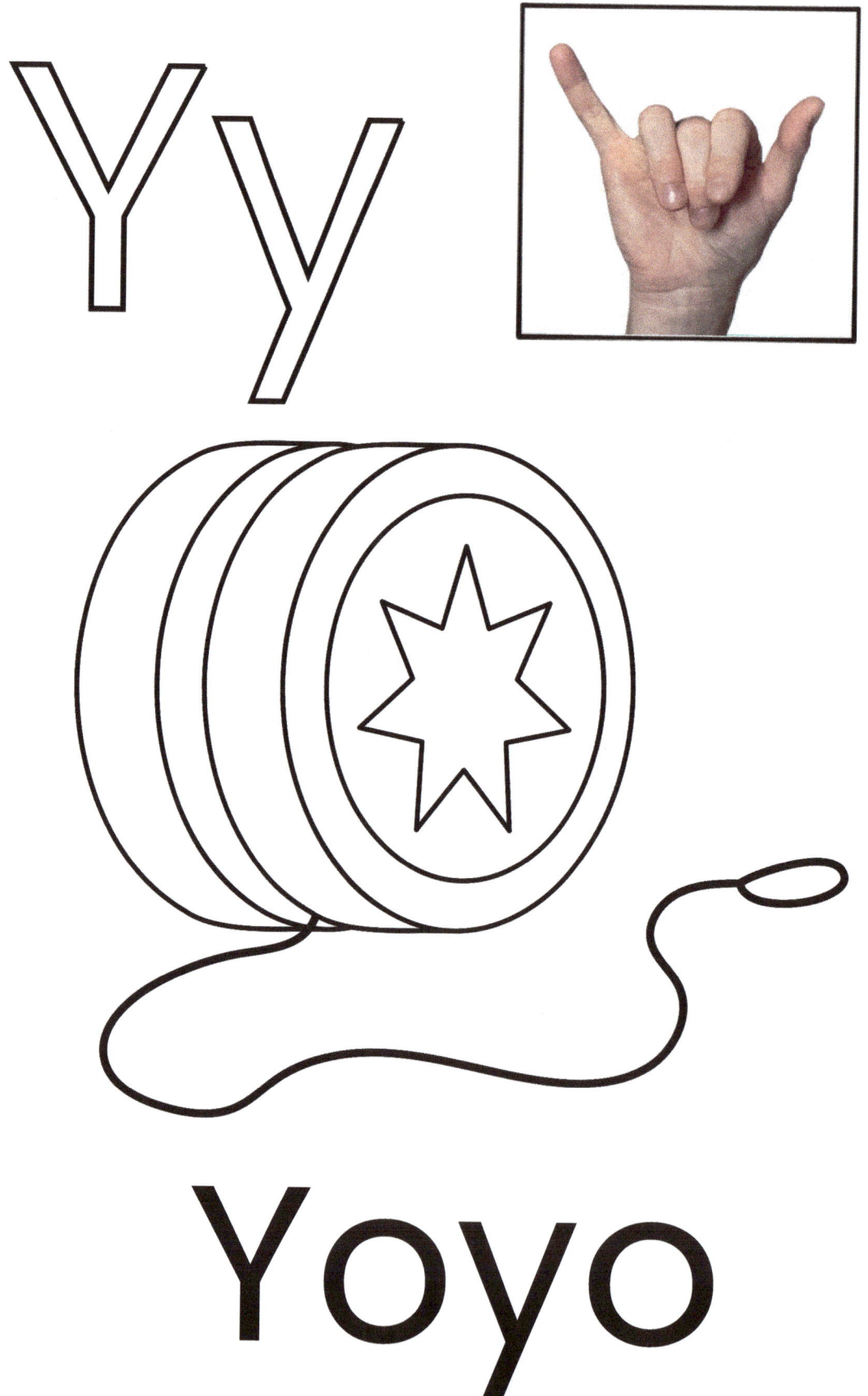

Yoyo

Z z

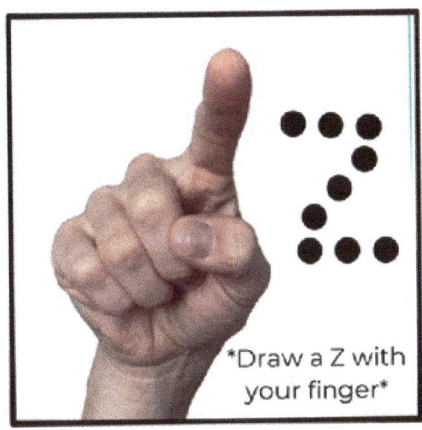

Draw a Z with your finger

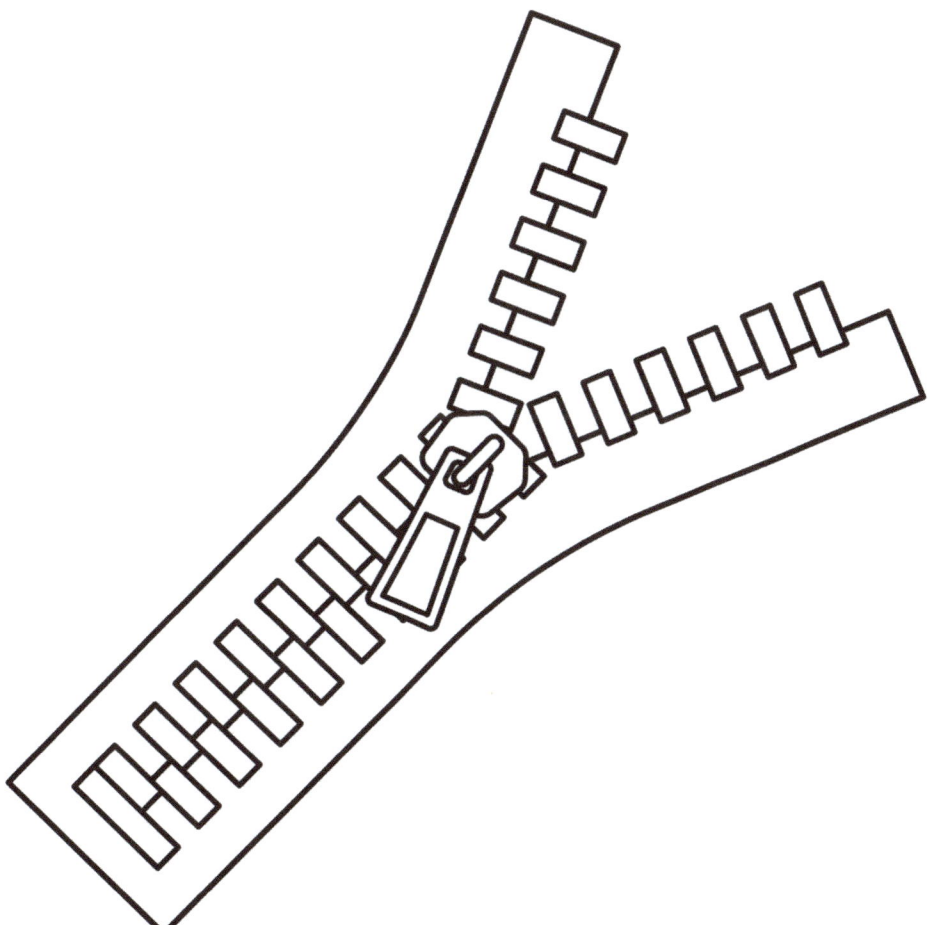

Zipper

Sign Language Memory Game

Print on cardstock, cut along dotted lines, and set
up for a fun and educational memory game.

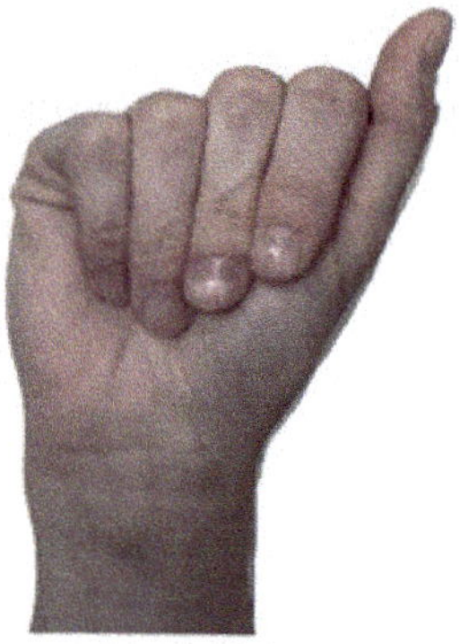

![ASL letter A hand sign]	# Aa
![ASL letter B hand sign]	# Bb
![ASL letter C hand sign]	# Cc

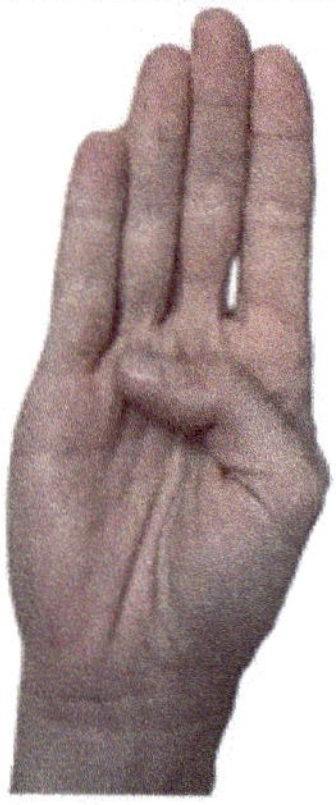

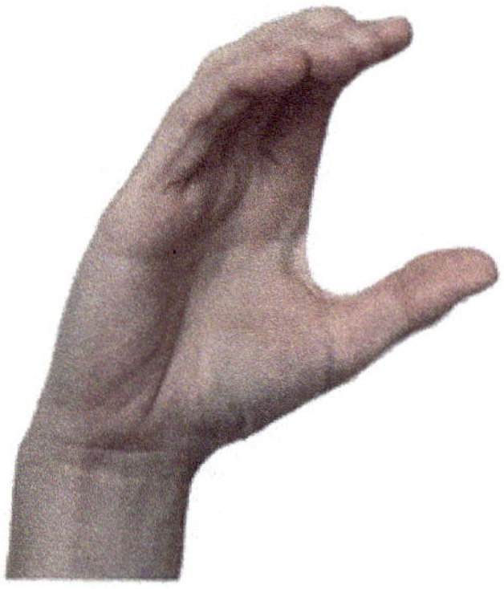

Sign Language Memory Game

Print on cardstock, cut along dotted lines, and set
up for a fun and educational memory game.

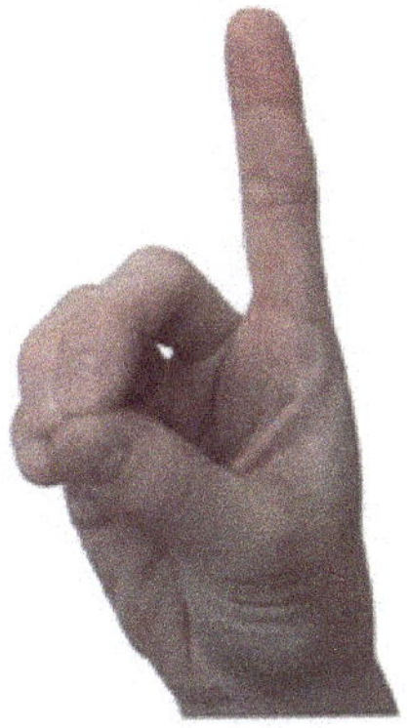	**Dd**
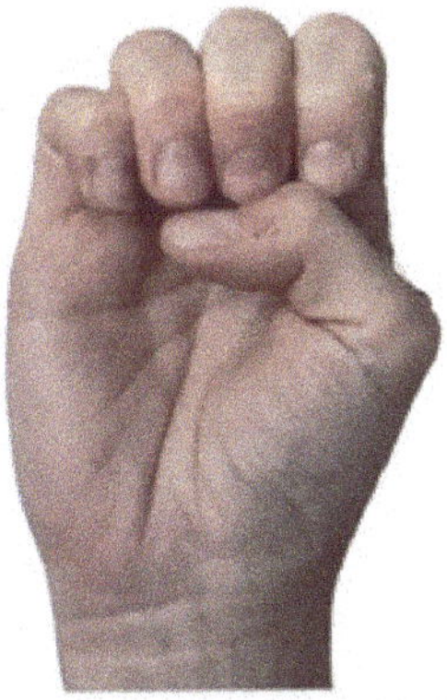	**Ee**
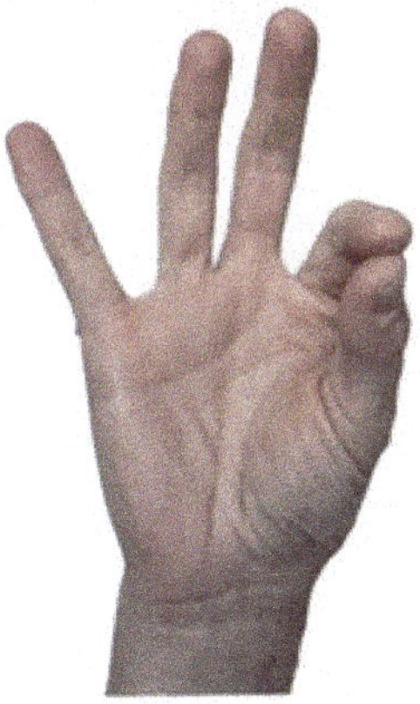	**Ff**

Sign Language Memory Game

Print on cardstock, cut along dotted lines, and set up for a fun and educational memory game.

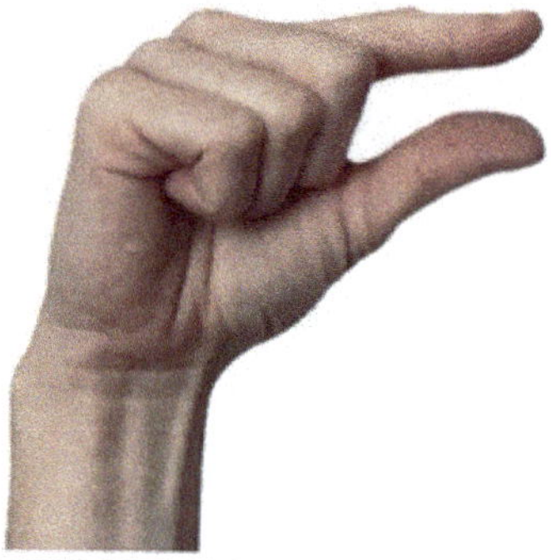

	Gg
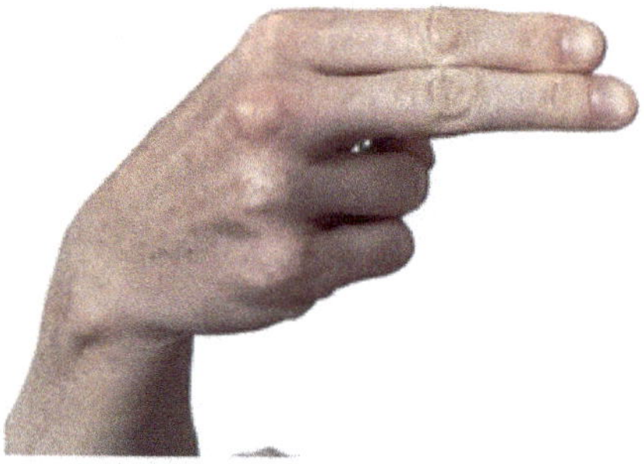	**Hh**
	**Ii**

Sign Language Memory Game

Print on cardstock, cut along dotted lines, and set
up for a fun and educational memory game.

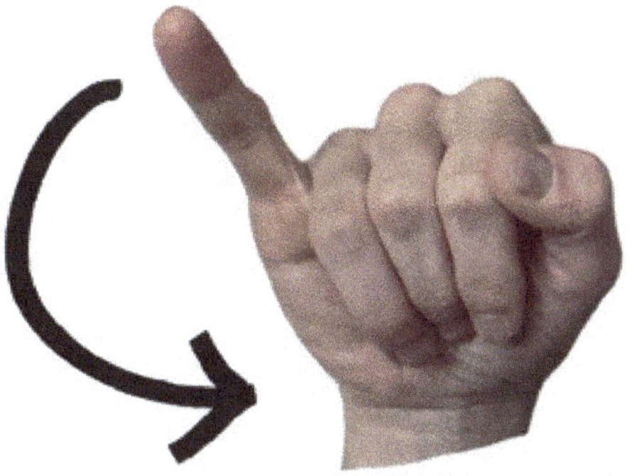	**Jj**
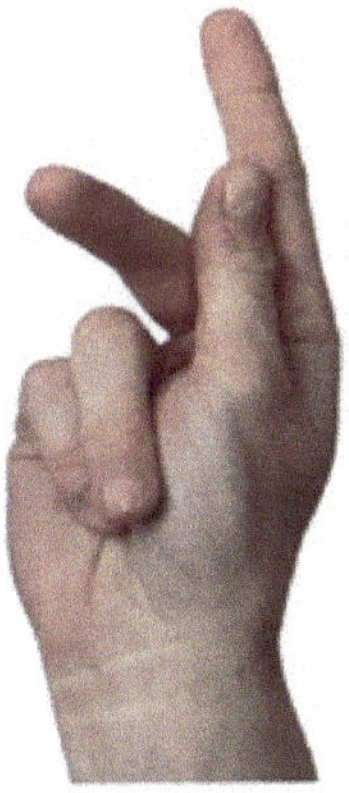	**Kk**
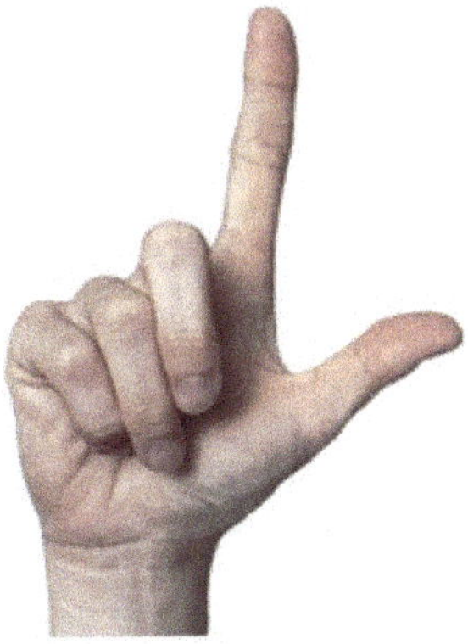	**Ll**

Sign Language Memory Game

Print on cardstock, cut along dotted lines, and set
up for a fun and educational memory game.

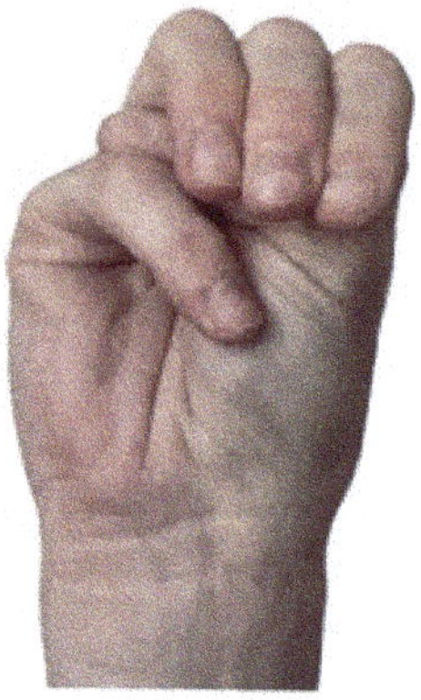	**Mm**
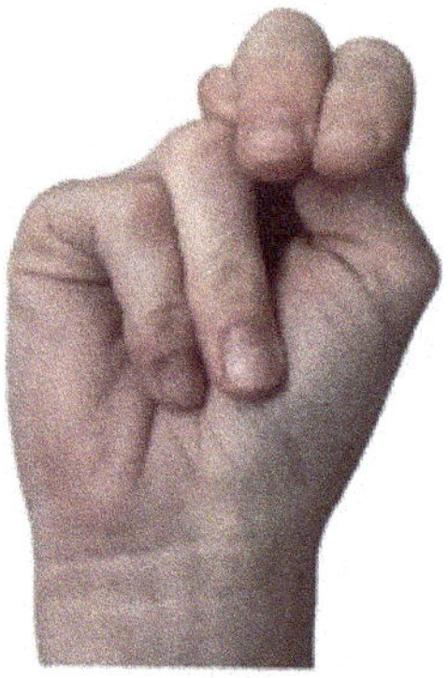	**Nn**
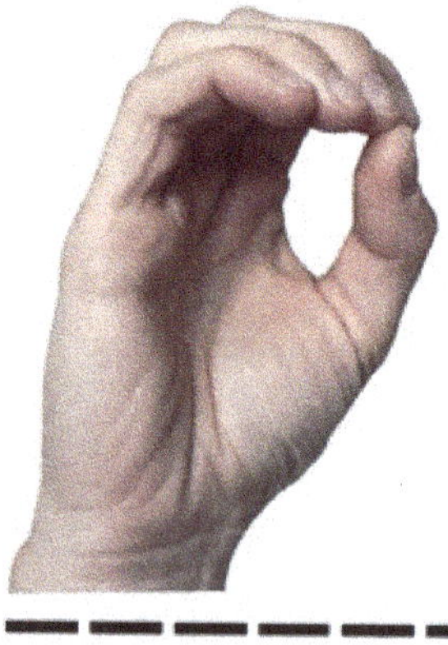	**Oo**

Sign Language Memory Game

Print on cardstock, cut along dotted lines, and set
up for a fun and educational memory game.

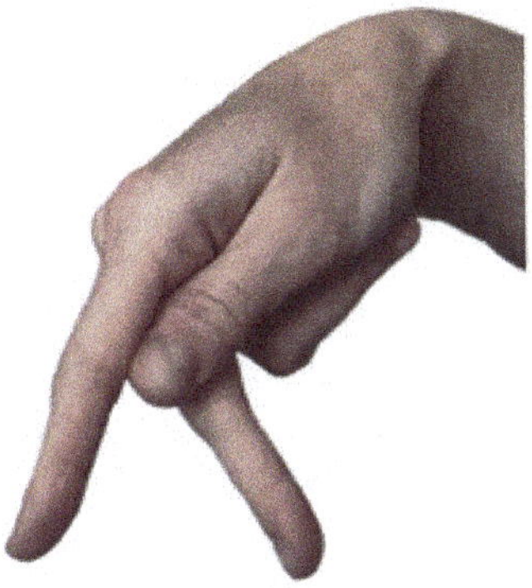	**Pp**
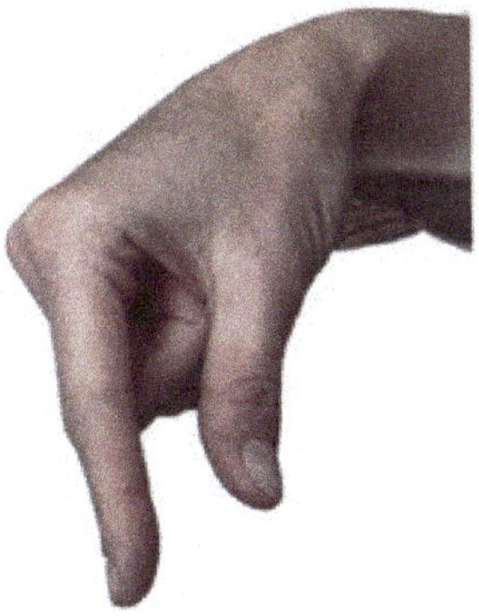	**Qq**
	**Rr**

Sign Language Memory Game

Print on cardstock, cut along dotted lines, and set up for a fun and educational memory game.

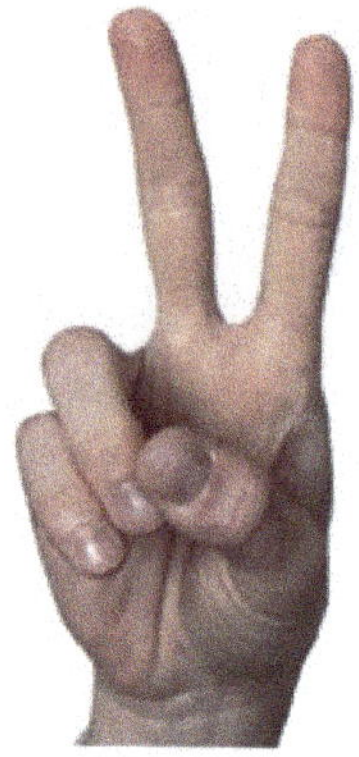

(sign for V)	**Vv**
(sign for W)	**Ww**
(sign for X)	**Xx**

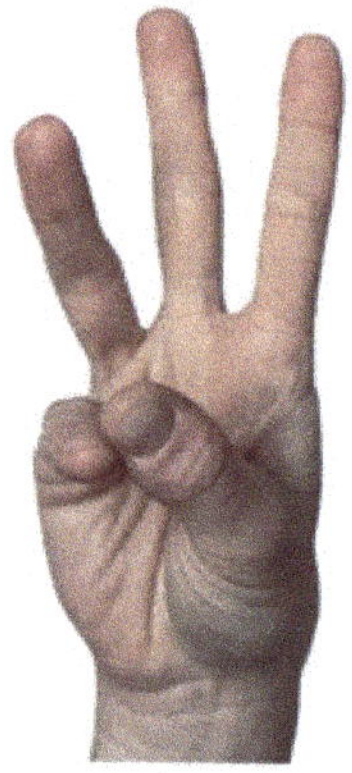

Sign Language Memory Game

Print on cardstock, cut along dotted lines, and set
up for a fun and educational memory game.

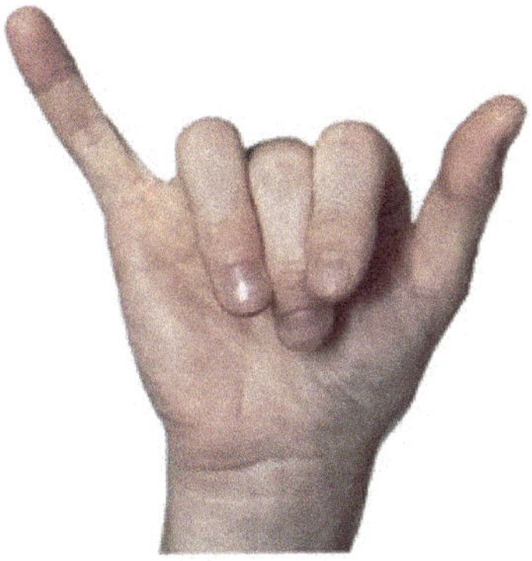

	Yy
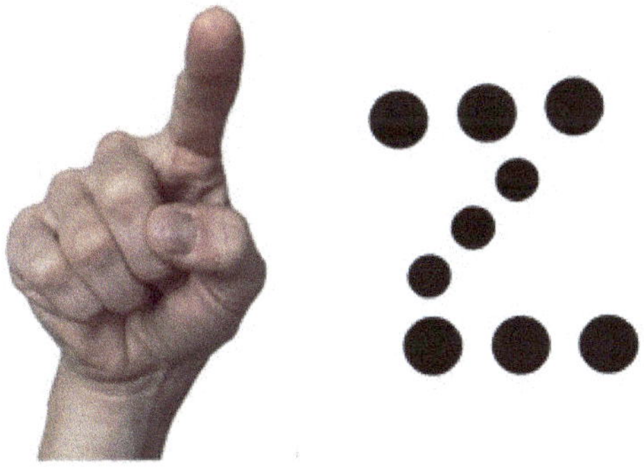	**Zz**

ACTIVITY

Create Your Own
Simple Signs
Lessons

TEMPLATES

WHAT'S THE ?

Attach the arrow using a pin.

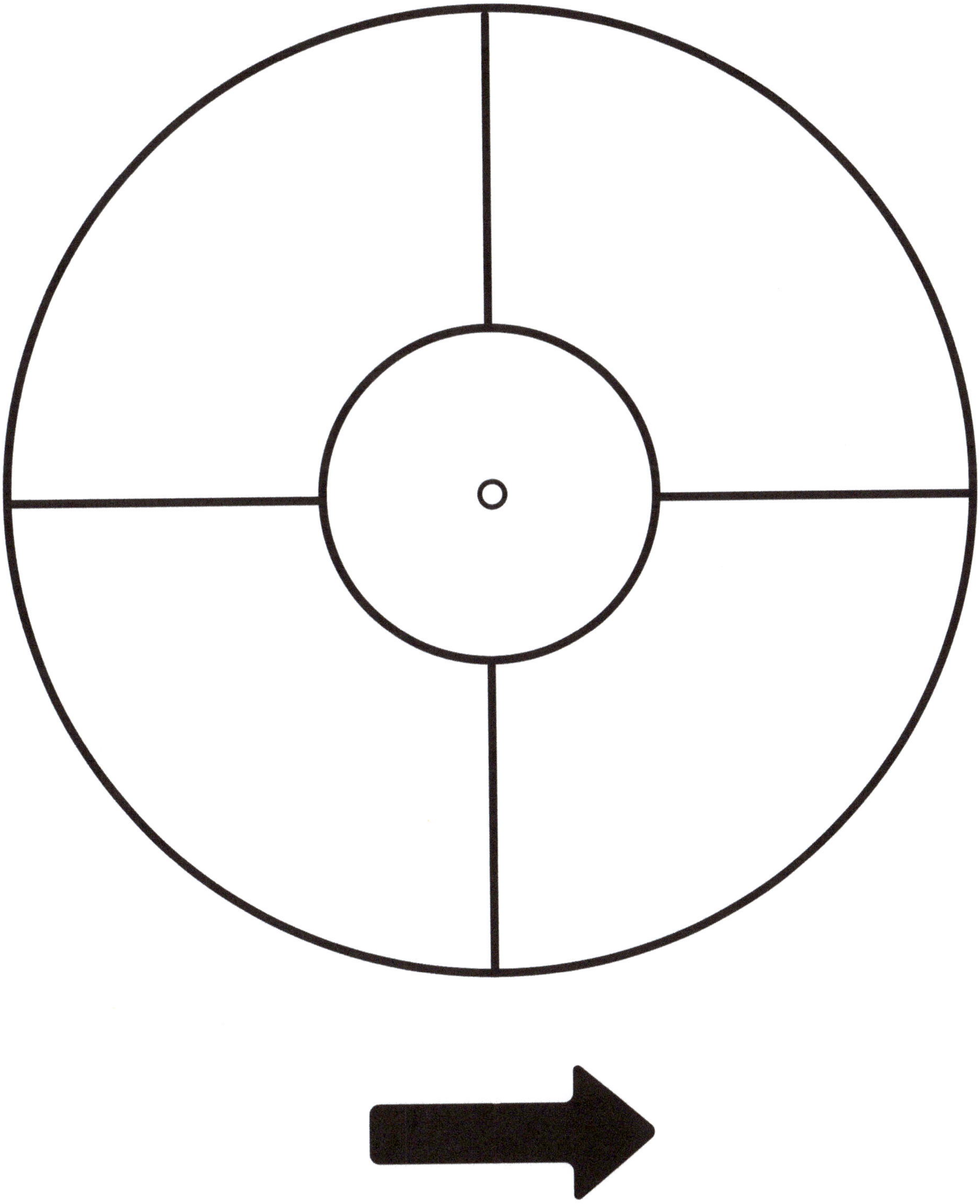

Sign and color!

MY FAVORITE

What is your favorite   ?
Draw it!

SIGNING courses

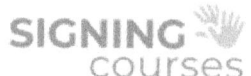

CUTTING OR TEARING PRACTICE

Use scissors to carefully cut along the lines or tear the paper.

WHAT'S THE SIGN?

Match the sign and the word

•⠀⠀⠀⠀⠀⠀⠀⠀⠀⠀•

•⠀⠀⠀⠀⠀⠀⠀⠀⠀⠀•

•⠀⠀⠀⠀⠀⠀⠀⠀⠀⠀•

•⠀⠀⠀⠀⠀⠀⠀⠀⠀⠀•

•⠀⠀⠀⠀⠀⠀⠀⠀⠀⠀•

•⠀⠀⠀⠀⠀⠀⠀⠀⠀⠀•

Signing Maze Game

Simple Signs Puzzles

Print, cut and start puzzling

BINGO

	FREE	

Instructions : Cut out calling cards and place in a bag or container. Draw out one card at a time and students will mark off their bingo board with a counter or marker.

Finish The Picture

Use your imagination to finish the rest of this

drawing of a

Use your imagination to finish the rest of this
drawing of a

I Know The Picture

Look at the sign. Circle the picture that matches
the sign. Then, you can color the picture.

SIGNING courses

The Magic of Simple Signing

CERTIFICATE

OF COMPLETION

—— this certificate is presented to ——

Simple Signs Educator

www.signingcourses.com

Jennifer Stewart M.S. Ed.

Writer, Educator, Curriculum Designer